JOURNAL IN GREENLAND:

BEING

EXTRACTS FROM A JOURNAL

KEPT IN THAT COUNTRY IN THE YEARS

1770 TO 1778.

By HANS EGEDE SAABYE,

Formerly Ordained Minister in the Districts
of Claushavn and Christianshaab
Now Minister of Udbye, in the
Bishopric of Fuhnen; and

GRANDSON OF THE CELEBRATED

HANS EGEDE.

IPI
press

Distributed by University Press of New England
Hanover and London

Reprint of 1818 edition

Cover photograph courtesy NASA, Visible Earth
Distributed by University Press of New England,
One Court Street, Lebanon, NH 03766
www.upne.com
Funded in part by
Greenland Home Rule Government, Nuuk

ISBN 978-0-9821703-0-4

International Polar Institute Press

Post Office Box 212
Hanover, NH 03755
USA

McGill University/ Arts Building
853 Sherbrooke St. West
Montreal, PQ H3A 2T6 Canada

Contents

Introduction

This missionary's account of my country, Greenland, through selected journal entries, provides the reader with not only a fascinating glimpse of Inuit life in the late 18th century, but also a visceral understanding of the huge differences between the two civilizations that continue to collide and shape my country.

This second printing of the book's English translation comes at a time, more than two centuries after it was written, when the two colliding civilizations have made a kind of new peace – one we Greenlanders voted on in a referendum – an agreement with Denmark on the ways in which a much more autonomous Greenland will be self-governed.

While most Greenlandic Inuit adopted the new religion brought to us by Hans Egede Saabye and his more celebrated grandfather, Hans Egede, and while we have inherited governance structures from our former colonizer, it is doubtful that in 2009 Greenlanders have been fully converted, or that their country has been turned upside down, as I have argued before, was the aim of the missionaries.

The reader will make no mistake that these accounts are the subjective, first-hand observations of a Dane, and a priest, who is very foreign to Greenlanders. At the same time, this book will take you on an unforgettable journey that illuminates much about my people. Hans Egede Saabye lays out spellbinding, personal stories of famine, murder, revenge, seduction, sorcery, kindness and forgiveness that help us Greenlanders understand the Danish people and its Christian ethic.

The book describes Greenland's physical, and sometimes harsh and unforgiving, environment. I grew up in the same Disko Bay area traversed by the missionary many times during his four-year stay in our country. The majestic, yet dangerous, icebergs described in his journal are identical to those that float by my home town of Aasiaat, which used to bear the Danish name of his missionary uncle (Egedesminde). These icebergs, so accurately described by him as beautiful houses and castles with gates, pillars and chimneys, continue today to plunge into the Disko Bay, breaking off the Greenland icecap and creating thunderous sounds that echo for miles throughout the region. His description of one of these icebergs exploding, and then crushing and drowning seven Inuit, was eerily similar to an experience I had while hunting near a giant iceberg that reminded me of the beautiful Sydney Opera House. When it suddenly exploded into tiny pieces, it produced an enormous wave that propelled me and my boat towards what I thought was an almost certain death.

This book is not meant to provide the reader with a true and complete analysis of how devastating the impact of the new religion has been on Greenland, and so I will not attempt to venture there in this introduction. Yet, while this book is no doubt full of true and fascinating stories, some of which portray Greenlanders to be cannibalistic and superstitious, I would remind the reader to remember the context of the times. While the missionary decries the execution of witches in Greenland, such executions occurred in Denmark too. Danes too believed in a God who was both malevolent and kind. They too believed that their God was both a spirit and a man. They believed, as we did, that there were two places of abode after death.

Despite the similarities, missionaries like Saabye saw our beliefs as evil. They pushed our angakkoks (shamans) aside and made them disappear, replacing them with priests of a foreign religion. They focused on the differences between us. Given that our supreme being, *Toornnaarsuk*, lived downward, under the earth with the "holiest" of our souls, rather than upward where Saabye's paradise was located, it was not hard to find a difference that could serve as a useful vehicle to literally turn our society upside down.

Given the context of the time, we Greenlanders must also forgive Saabye as an individual, "for he knew not what he did." It is not known whether or not Saabye had doubts, as Greenland's first missionary had just before his death when he asked himself whether attempting to convert Greenlanders had been the right thing to do. What we do know, however, as this book shows, is that the younger missionary was a compassionate man. His journal entries reveal a man who sought justice and fairness as he knew it. Saabye often risked his life in helping others. He also acknowledged his own moral anguish when disagreeing with his superiors back in Denmark. When a believing Greenlander with two wives requested baptism, Saabye responded with regret, "I wish to baptize you; but ... my masters in our country have forbidden me."

Among the journal entries, you will see the contradiction of missionary work – how it strives to help those in need and does so with compassion, yet how it also contributes to exploitation and negative cultural change. Saabye describes this paradox himself, perhaps unknowingly, by first observing how the Greenlanders, "without magistrates, without laws, they live in peace and harmony: you never hear a dispute about property, never a reproach made to him who has unawares done another an injury". And then how traders – whose marketplace is always prepared by a missionary who goes before them – take unfair advantage of the Greenlander: "The uninitiated could only guess at the profits, which, in the manner that the trade was managed, must have been considerable....to say nothing of the risk of trade in such a dangerous sea: but the Greenlanders paid a great deal more for their goods, and this more was too much." A poignant example showing how traders took advantage of the Greenlanders' propensity for peace and harmony is contained in one journal entry noting, "some were silent, others laughed" when they discovered that the blubber they were trading was being measured in tubs with holes in them. The missionary added, "I do not exaggerate, but affirm that the Greenlanders, in my time, paid for their guns in this manner."

Despite the fact that these accounts of Greenland come from the pen of an outsider, this book accurately describes in many instances our own demons, both figurative and literal – some of which continue to impact our lives today. While we do not, today, kill our illisiitsoqs (wicked sorcerers) and then eat their hearts so their ghosts do not return, as Hans Egede Saabye reported, we Greenlanders do today, however, sometimes kill the uniqueness and initiative of individuals who do not completely fit into the norms of our society.

Saabye also says that "Greenlanders are much too careless about the future." While this bold assertion betrays Saabye's lack of full understanding of a hunter, his environment, and his daily obligations to his family, the missionary's observation about carelessness is still worth reflecting on today. We Greenlanders are now faced with difficult environmental and economic choices – whether to build an aluminum smelter or fully exploit the oil resources or rich uranium we have discovered. My hope is that we are not careless, but take the very long term into consideration so our children's children can continue to benefit from the riches of one of the most pristine countries in the world. I believe that our recent "yes" vote in the referendum on self-government does show that we look to the future, and it is my hope that we are not careless about it.

In my many years of political work, I have dedicated myself to fighting for greater autonomy for Greenland from our former colonizer and have at the same time strongly promoted, through the Inuit Circumpolar Council, the unity of Inuit from Greenland, Canada, Alaska and Russia. In both these endeavours, it has become clear to me that bridge-building is a necessary skill that one must employ often and with cultural sensitivity. As Saabye repeatedly shows, the Greenlanders he knew had a natural inclination to reach out, compromise, and sometimes adopt change that was offered them. He wrote, "their religion does not hinder them from embracing Christianity," and "the inhabitants of one place live in mutual friendship, and share their goods with each other." It was perhaps with these characteristics as our guide that we voted to take a much larger step towards full autonomy from Denmark, yet at the same time retain a Danish presence in our country. "Liberty and equality are the property of the Greenlanders," wrote Hans Egede Saabye.

As Greenlanders today move with healthy optimism into tomorrow, we take with us the knowledge of our past, including our angakkoks and illisiitsoqs, our colonial history, our old religion and our new one. As we look forward, we can never forget the collision of civilizations that we endured due to colonialism, including its facets of economic exploitation and religious change. I believe, however, that despite the attempts of missionaries, our society was not turned upside down. In context, this book helps to explain this and helps us understand where Greenland is positioned today.

Aqqaluk Lynge
February 2009

Aqqaluk Lynge is the president of the Greenland chapter of the Inuit Circumpolar Council, chair of the Greenland Writers Association, and a former minister in the Greenland Home Rule Government.

JOURNAL IN GREENLAND.

**The miles mentioned in the following pages are German miles, equal to about four and a half English miles. The ells are Danish ells, of two feet English, nearly.*

Chapter I.

The Isefjord, in Disco Bay.

This remarkable gulph extends between the tracts of land in which the colonies of Claush-avn and Jakobshavn are situated. It is from five to six miles long, and from a quarter to half a mile in breadth. It is said that, in former times, it was free from iceberg's, and was navigable; nay, old Greenlanders even relate, after a tradition of their forefathers, that at times it was possible to navigate upon it to the east side of the country, between the rows of mountains which are now covered with eternal ice. They even relate, that, in later times, a piece of square timber was driven down, between these mountains, from the east side, and that it was used as a beam in a house. If this were true, it would certainly prove that there was formerly a passage through the gulph, from the east to the west side, which has since been stopped up by icebergs [1]. The ridge of mountains itself, which extends along the country, and divides the east side from the west, has been long since a boundless ocean of ice, which, at a distance, seems to blend with the clouds. The ice increases every year; but the large quantity of snow which falls in the winter is melted by the sun in summer, flows down in streams, and makes dangerous opening's in the ice, in which the Greenlanders, in pursuit of the reindeer, often find their grave. When this ice projects over the water, it breaks by its own weight, and falls into the bay, hence the terribly magnificent mass of icebergs which I attempt to describe.

When such a piece of ice falls, the noise may be heard at the distance of many miles: it rebounds several times before it recovers its equilibrium, and frequently brings up prodigious stones with it from the bottom. The whole bay is in commotion; the water swells and roars; the mountains burst asunder, with a loud crash, and tumble about in a terrible manner, till they either obtain a firm footing, or roll farther. The sea is covered, to the distance of several miles, with drift ice, which impedes the navigation. On such occasions, the swelling of the water often lifts up the greater part of the icebergs, and carries them, with incredible rapidity, farther out into the bay, or even into the open sea. Here they often appear to us like ships, which approach the land under full sail: we are deceived, and deceived again, and yet, so great is the resemblance, we remain standing, with joyful expectation, till they change their course, and show themselves, on another side, in their true shape. If a person who has never seen this bay were to exert his imagination to the utmost, he would not be able to form a just idea of it. Conceive a tract of so many miles in extent, full of icebergs, so large that they reach 200 or 300 fathoms below the surface of the sea. They look as if they would bid defiance to time, and yet they are deceitful as water. In sailing by, you see houses, castles, gates, windows, chimnies, &c. It is a very agreeable illusion, as long as we do not know how dangerous it is to approach them; but even when we know this danger, we take pleasure in looking at them. I saw, among other magnificent buildings, the great gate of the Palace of Christianburg, with its pillars and side doors; and my eye dwelt on the mezzanine story, which was astonishingly resembling. As these masses of ice, accordingly as they are formed of sweet or salt water, are white, blue, or green [2], this difference of colours heightens the illusion, particularly when it is assisted by the powerful beams of the sun. These masses of ice have an attractive power, to which the stream doubtless contributes in a great degree, so that even large ships are in danger of being driven against them, if they do not take care, in time, to keep at a proper distance. The Greenlanders are very familiar with them, though many lose their lives by their confidence; but as the seals like to be near them, the Greenlanders must follow them thither, and seek food or death. The echo is so very strong among the icebergs, that, not only when you speak as you sail by them, you hear your words plainly re-echoed from the top; but the latter, when it is rotten, as they call it there, is so shaken by the sound, that it falls down; and woe then to him who is near it! The following accident happened while I was in Greenland: A women's boat passed from my side of the bay to the other; the people in the boat exhorted each other, as usual, as they approached the icebergs, not to speak, and did not suffer the oars to make any noise; but a young-lad wantonly struck with a piece of wood on the skin stretched over the boat. The sound was propagated in a few moments to the top of a rotten iceberg; the latter fell down, and all the people in the boat, seven in number, were drowned [3].

In Greenland, and particularly in Disco Bay, where the Isefjord lies [4], it is notorious, that every sound, whether of speaking or other noise, under an iceberg, is quickly propagated to its summit, from which it is returned with a loud echo. It is equally notorious, that when such a mountain, either by the effects of the sun, or by revolutions in the bay, has become brittle, or, as they call it in that country, rotten, the summit of it is broken off by the vibration of the sound, falls down, and dashes to pieces whatever is under or near it. I have, myself, frequently spoken under icebergs when they seemed sound, and admired the uncommonly loud echo. I always escaped happily; and though I saw such tops of icebergs fall down, I never saw them fall upon any body. But the case is unhappily not so rare. Not only the abovementioned seven persons perished in this manner, but single Greenlanders also, who went there in pursuit of seals, and fired their guns under these icebergs, without first examining whether they seemed to be rotten: that the seven persons lost their lives by the abovementioned sound, and the fall of the summit occasioned by it, was told us by a Greenlander who had accompanied the women's boat in his Kajak, and being in the neighbourhood, though not quite close to the women's boat, or under the iceberg itself, had been witness of the action of the boy, and of the misfortune that ensued.

When the Greenlanders travel in their women's boats, they generally have one or two attendants in Kajaks, partly because it does not become them as men to sit idle in a women's boat, and still less to row the boat, which is the women's business, and partly in order to catch a seal on the way, if an opportunity should offer. Only the master of the family is in the boat as steersman; the rest are, as already said, in their Kajaks. But if they make a voyage over the

Isefjord, they have always a Kajak with them, the proper business of which is to reconnoitre the bays and the icebergs, to examine where there are openings in these icebergs, that is shorter ways, and whether these are so broad that they can venture to row through them. It was in such an opening, or icy vault, that the abovementioned women's boat perished, but solely by the imprudence committed; for, according to the report of the Kajak rower, the opening was broad enough to pass through. The pieces of ice floating in the bay often cut holes in the women's boat: we aft first stop them up with fat, and row on, but the holes may become so numerous (I once had nine in my boat), that the water pours in, and then it is necessary to go on shore to sew up these holes. While this is doing, or when they go on shore in the evening to put up tents, the boat is turned upside down, yet not quite with the keel uppermost, but with one side a little raised from the ground, and supported by a kind of props or forks [5], the pointed end of which is fixed in the ground; and but more delicate, and much fatter, than the common ones. The Greenlanders catch them with lines, which they make of whalebone. The fishing place is always surrounded with iceberg's, but sometimes the latter stand like lofty buildings round a market place. There a great many people assemble; those who live at a distance come to purchase, and the fishermen sell. It is quite a fair! Every iceberg threatens them with death, and yet they are as cheerful and secure as if no danger was near. I once visited their market. The fishing place was very large, the ice thick, and the number of people assembled very great. They had already been fishing above eight days in this place, and the surrounding icebergs did not seem rotten. I was delighted with their cheerfulness and activity, and at their trade. They fished and caught in my presence, that I might see how they proceeded. Some lent me their lines, with which I measured the depth, and I found it in several places, as mentioned above, from two to three hundred fathoms. After staying about two hours, I left them, because it grew late, and I had three quarters of a mile to go home. Not half an hour after I had left them, an iceberg near the fish market fell down, broke the ice to pieces, and deprived several fishermen of their lines and fish. Some fell into the water, were crushed between the pieces of ice, and severely injured. The greatest part of them escaped uninjured, although they departed with empty hands. I should scarcely have been saved had I been still there, because every one had enough to do to save himself. Besides, we Europeans are not so skilful as the Greenlanders in jumping from one piece of ice to another, or, when we fall into the water, in climbing up again.

It may easily be supposed, that such a prodigious number of icebergs, by the cold which proceeds from them, must make the air near them much more raw, than it is, even much farther to the north. I lived half a mile from them: when a mountain fell in ruins, I heard the noise like loud peals of thunder; I daily saw these icebergs, and felt the effects of their neighbourhood. When I returned home from Christianshaab, which lies four miles more to the south, the tears flowed from my eyes for cold, even at Whitsuntide, when my back was in a perspiration.

Chapter II.

The Mission at Claushavn is extended.

When I came to Greenland, only my colony of Claushavn was provided with a Catechist. He was a Dane, and, perhaps, the ablest in the whole country. In Christianshaab, on the contrary, where, besides the married Danes, who had many children, two or three Greenland families lived, they made shift with an old married Danish sailor, who had lost an eye in his youth, in a drunken affray, and had broken one thigh. It may easily be supposed, that his instructions and the fruits of them were nothing extraordinary. I, therefore, considered of means to supply this want. As soon as my acquaintance with the Greenlanders and their language in some measure permitted it, I endeavoured to qualify a young Greenlander to become a national Catechist, and allowed him a certain salary. After he was employed, things went on better, and, by practice, instruction, and encouragement, better and better still. This successful attempt induced me to instruct some more of the young men of my place of abode, who seemed to have the clearest heads, in order to place them among the heathens, where the latter dwelt, for when the heathens asked for instruction, though Claushavn was a thriving place, yet they wished, in general, to remain at their usual abode, rather than remove to the colony: to gratify their wishes in this respect, was removing an obstacle, and was in itself just and reasonable.

In this manner, I sent, some years after-wards, a national Catechist to some families, who settled a quarter of a mile to the north of me. The Catechist, who was the son of a deceased Dane of mixed race, was tolerably clever, and could dedicate the greatest part of his time to his office, because he had not much success in fishing; but it was necessary, on this account, to give him a larger salary, that he might not suffer want, and from want become indifferent to his office. Two years after this, a family which lived a quarter of a mile farther north, wanted a teacher. I promised to fulfil their wish, but as I did not know whether I might depend upon their perseverance, or on the participation of several families in the instruction, and, besides, the way was not farther,

I prevailed on the same Catechist to undertake the instruction of this family also. In the morning, he instructed the first mentioned families; and in the evening the latter; but I was obliged to give him an addition to his salary, in consideration of this increase of his labour. Afterwards, more families applied; and as long as I was in Greenland, and could pay attention to it, this method went on very well; but whether it continued after my departure, I do not know, for almost a year elapsed before my successor arrived. My neighbour Provost Sverdrup had indeed promised me to do his utmost, and punctually kept his word; but his own Mission employed him so fully, that he very seldom came to mine, and, when he did come, he had not time enough to see after every thing. It is, therefore, possible that this last arrangement, for want of being attended to has ceased; perhaps even before my successor arrived. Happily I did not baptize anybody, either here or at Tussangme [6].

I must add a few words about this island, the real name of which is Tussak, which lies six miles from Claushavn. In my pastoral journeys, I sometimes went there, and that with the more pleasure, because some families lived there, among whom was a Polygamist, who always liked to hear my conversation. These families once asked me for a teacher: I had one in readiness, but, when I proposed to him to go there, he felt no inclination. He said the island was too far off, &c; I was, therefore, obliged to ask my national Catechist at Christianshaab, to undertake it. He consented, and resided a week alternately at each place, but on the condition of receiving an addition to his salary.

I engaged these national Catechists on my own account, and also paid them the first year myself. The Missionary College approved of my proposal, and also repaid me the money I had laid out, as far as I ventured to make it known but this College was, however, very sparing with its salary, and not inclined to give Danish provisions, especially bread, which is so great an inducement to these men to lead a sedentary life, so different from that to which they are accustomed. If, therefore, I wished to have them do any thing, I was obliged to give them what the College refused.

Chapter III.

It is still possible to come to the East Side of Greenland.

The Icelanders landed early, perhaps about the year 982, on the east side of Greenland; and, finding the country agreeable, they afterwards visited it, and settled there. In process of time the population increased; and, by their diligence, not only procured subsistence, but even had articles for exportation. Numerous communities, churches, convents, and bishops' sees, arose there. Even in the southern part of the west side, there were many villages and churches, of which some remains are still shown. The inhabitants tilled the land, and, besides other kinds of grain, are said to have raised the finest wheat. The pastures were rich, and fed numbers of oxen and sheep, which supplied milk, butter, and cheese, not only in great abundance, but of such excellent quality, that the royal kitchen, at Drontheira, was supplied with them. There were forests there, in which were hares and other game; and lakes well stocked with fish. It is, there-fore, no wonder that this side of the country became, in a few years, so populous as it is stated to have been.

According to ancient accounts, the Icelander, Erik the Red, or Redhead, was the first who discovered the east side of Greenland, and landed there. In an old Latin history book, which was lent to me in Greenland for a short time, this Erik is said, properly, to have fled thither, because he had killed his adversary in a duel; but that he was afterwards reconciled with the relations of the deceased; and, as he could now sail, unmolested, backwards and forwards, he induced many families to accompany him thither. The following [7] anecdote, which I took from this book, has its place here: Erik, probably he who is beforementioned, arrived, with his wife, who was pregnant, on the east coast. He first built a hut, and supported himself and his wife by the chase. He always returned home in the evening, as well out of tenderness for his wife, as to prepare every thing for her approaching delivery, and for the winter, which was at hand. One evening, when he came home, he found his wife dead, and a new-born male infant crying at her breast. He stood for a few moments as if petrified. The cries of the child roused him from his stupor; but irresolute, and almost in despair, he knows not how he shall preserve its tender life. Soon, however, he collected himself; took a small sharp-pointed instrument, and pricked his breast round the nipples, so as to draw blood; then he put the child to his breast; it sucked eagerly, and thus obtained sustenance. He was now forced to remain, for the most part, with the child; and repeated the operation as often as it required food. By degrees, the blood became milky, and, at last, real milk. In this manner he suckled his son, of whom he became extremely fond, and who grew up to be an active and courageous man, as his father had been. I regret that the title page of this book was torn off. The book had every appearance of high antiquity, and, in my opinion, of historical credibility: it contained many very interesting, and (to me at least) unknown notices of Iceland, and, particularly, of the population and fertility of the east side of Greenland.

It is uncertain by what particular cause the navigation to this fine part of the country, and, at the same time, all connection between the inhabitants and the mother country, ceased. It cannot have been what is called the black death, for the navigation continued long after this plague. Troubles, arising from war, may have interrupted it for some years; but it can scarcely be believed that it could have been neglected in more peaceable times; because it afforded important advantages, and the inhabitants of the two countries were united by the ties of friendship and affinity. There is, indeed, a general tradition, that the natives of the country, at that time called Skroellinger [8], fell upon the new inhabitants, and extirpated them (so the descendants of the former, namely, the Greenlanders, relate the story); but to me this appears improbable. The ancient Norwegians and Icelanders were tall, stout, and warlike; the Greenlanders, on the other hand, were little, cowardly, or, at least, not accustomed to combat. Neither could they well expect a successful result even from a surprise, because the population was so great; for, that they should have ventured on open war is what I cannot imagine. But, supposing that they attacked, by surprise, and destroyed the Europeans on the west coast of the country, where they were not numerous, yet those on the east side must have been taught, by the misfortune of their countrymen, to be on their guard, particularly as they were not only informed of it, but are even stated to have come to their assistance: the history, indeed, says, that they came too late, and found only cattle running about the fields without a master. In whatever manner this extirpation was effected, it took place first on the west and afterwards on the east side [9]. Only a few remains of the ancient Icelanders are said still to exist on the east coast. The tradition has been preserved from ancient to modern times; when some Greenlanders affirmed that they had seen tall, bearded men, who were terrible, and, doubtless, man-eaters; others said they had been so far to the east, that they had seen the sun rise from the sea, and that they saw people in the country. Torfceus relates, in his Historia Gronlandica, that the Icelandic bishop, Amund, in a voyage from Norway to Iceland, was driven, by a storm, to the coast of Greenland, and sailed along the coast, where he plainly distinguished people driving their sheep and lambs on the meadows. This voyage must have taken place about the year 1540, and the east coast must then have been inhabited, though the intercourse with the mother country was broken off. If we may believe all this, we may conjecture that descendants of those robust Icelanders and Norwegians are still to be found there. But were this not the case, the country, however, remains; and this must still be, what it was formerly, a fine, fertile country, worth looking for, and, if possible, settling in.

Many fruitless expeditions and voyages have been undertaken with this view, from time to time, under our kings, from Christian III to Christian VII, under whose reign the last attempt was made. Our present King, then Crown Prince, promoted this expedition, and, as far as I know, bore the expense of it. Two ships were fitted out, and wintered in Iceland. Repeated attempts were made: they sailed along the ice, as well to the south as to the north; were exposed to many dangers, once even to total shipwreck; but saw no possibility of approaching the coast, respecting which the particulars are contained in Egede's Journal, 1789. However, this last account of the voyage to East Greenland gives (as well as more ancient accounts) hints of the possibility of some time or other attaining the end proposed. The ice is terrible, but does lie fast; is not every year alike, does not come at the same time, or in the same quantity, it changes its position; nay, it is pretended it was once found to have wholly vanished. May happy times one day return to our country! Who would not then be allowed to hope for another attempt to rediscover East Greenland? It would, indeed, require considerable expense, but if it succeeded, the advantage reaped by it would be great: at least we should acquire the country, which many would be glad to acquire, if an opportunity offered.

The attempts, like some earlier ones, must be undertaken from Iceland. Two small copper bottomed vessels must remain there, not one, but two or three winters, from the beginning of spring, and as long as the season allowed, they must reconnoitre. They need not, indeed, keep the sea all the time; but, as the passage from Iceland thither is said to be but forty miles, they might sail over to the ice several times; coast along it, northwards and southwards; and observe the situation of it, and the changes that might have taken place between one trip and another. Accounts of this, as well as of the whole enterprise, must be sent in, every autumn, by the trading vessels. If this were continued, as I wish, for three years, perhaps the object would be obtained, and then all the expense and all the dangers would be forgotten. But, even supposing that we could not get thither, we should obtain greater certainty respecting the coming, the situation, and the changes, &c. of the ice. In short, we should obtain some degree of certainty respecting the possibility, or the impossibility of getting to East Greenland on this side.

But, even should these attempts be wholly fruitless, we must not yet give up the country as lost. There remains still a possibility left, which would, indeed, require time, but would be less expensive, less dangerous, and more promising. We had already, in my time, colonies far to the south on the west side, which we inhabited. If the Government would make an arrangement, that, every second or third year, a new colony should be established, always some miles farther to the south, we should, in time, reach Statenhook, then go beyond it, and so in the same manner up the east side. As the colonists advanced, they must endeavour, by trade, if any opportunity offered, and by their own industry, to make good a part of the expenses of the undertaking; but the main object, that of examining the nature of the country, and to obtain certain information respecting its population, its fertility, the ice, &c, must not be forgotten.

As the currents always flow outwards, and partly keep the ice at some distance from the shore, it would doubtless be possible to proceed, in small vessels, between the coast and the ice, and for one colony to assist another, where larger vessels cannot approach; for it can hardly be doubted but that supplies might be annually sent from the mother country to the most southerly of the eastern colonies. This method of gradually approaching the end in view would have this advantage, that report would precede the new comers, would so far make them known, and prepare the inhabitants to receive them.

By one or other of the methods here pointed out, I consider the re-discovery of the east coast to be possible, without any great expense to the state. I am almost convinced that it will be one day found, and that one of these projects, or perhaps both united, will lead to the accomplishment of this wish. Happy the man for whom the decrees of Providence have reserved this discovery [11].

Chapter IV.

The Polygamist.

To take more wives than one at the same time, is not indeed very common in Greenland, but not absolutely uncommon. A man who loves change, and is so skilful in fishing, that he can support more than one, sometimes takes two wives; nay, a few miles from my place of abode, there was a man who had three. The first wife is always the most respected, and properly the mistress of the family, if she is not the most loved. If she has borne her husband children, particularly sons, she is sure of his continued respect; but if she is barren, she must behave with great prudence towards him, and with good humour to the other wives, not only to preserve her precedence, but even to avoid being repudiated. These women often agree very well; but if the reverse is the case, a black undertaken, in order to convince himself, that nothing was neglected that might tend to ensure success. But his proposal, and his petition to the king, for what reason is not known, were laid on one side. (*See Life of H. Egede, by J. J. Lund.*)

Among the inhabitants of Tussangme, there was, as I have said, a Polygamist. This man, who was the ablest of the whole, was always very eager, when I came, to hear something about our country. I fulfilled his wish, and endeavoured, as usual, to direct his thoughts to the great Creator. "Kaf Kaf Pelesse! [12] Usomakau!

i.e. Go on, Priest! He is glorious, and worthy of praise," exclaimed he. "Send us a teacher; we will be obedient, we will all be obedient." "If I can be certain that you are serious," I replied, "I will with pleasure look out a teacher for you, and visit you myself as often as I can." "We are quite serious," said he.

"When you have been here, we talk of what you have told us; we will acknowledge the Great Being, who is so good." I did not say a word on this occasion of his two wives; it would have been wholly misplaced, and have destroyed his good intention. I persuaded, as I have before said, the national Catechist at Christianshaab to divide his time, and to go there every other week. I accompanied him the first time he went, presented him to them as their teacher, and exhorted them to be attentive to his instructions. They promised it, and kept their word. Every time that I came, I had reason to be satisfied with their diligence and conduct, in which the Polygamist encouraged them. I wrote on account of this man to the Missionary college, and represented, that as it seemed as if the apostles, when any had two wives before they were converted to Christianity, had, in this case, connived at it, I wished to have permission to baptize him; but I received for answer, that this permission could not be granted, especially on account of the consequences. One day, towards the end of the second winter, he asked me, "You will baptize me, Priest?" "I would do it with pleasure," I replied, " but you have two wives." "What!" exclaimed he, hastily, "cannot I then become a believer?" "You know," said I, "that the great Lord in heaven created only one man and one woman, to show that only two such should live together in wedlock." "You grieve me, Priest." He cried, and pointed to his second wife, "Can I reject her? She has borne me sons, and how can I abandon these little ones?" "You shall continue," said I, "to provide for them all, but abstain from conjugal intercourse with your second wife." "That is difficult," answered he. "Will the good God reject me, because I cannot reject her? You know that I wish to become a believer. You know, too, that I know him, and that I live like a believer." "Yes," I answered, "I know all this, and I wished to baptize you; but, besides what I have already said to you, my masters in our country have forbidden me." I unwillingly said this, and he heard it with some displeasure. "Do you not think, Priest," continued he, "that the great Master of heaven is more benevolent than those in your country?" "Certainly, he is," continued I: "he is all goodness: he judges differently from man, because he knows the heart better." "I wish to be a believer, and I dare not!" said he, affected: "but I will continue to obey God, and to avoid evil; and I hope that he will not reject me when I die." I affirmed this, took his hand, and looked at him, with emotion. It was a short time before I returned home. "God in heaven," said I, "thy Father, and my Father, and the Father of us all, be merciful to thee, for Jesus Christ's sake, here and for ever!" "Be happy, Priest," answered he, with tears: "before the good God in heaven I shall see thee again!" "Yes, there we shall meet again in happiness," said I, and went away. He accompanied me in silence to the shore, and long followed me with his eyes.

Chapter V.

Greenland Courtship.

Decorum requires that a girl must not choose to marry, and that the parents must not give their consent to the marriage of their daughters: but then, the young men carry off their girls by force. Some friends accompany the suitor into the house of the parents, and carry off the girl, without ceremony, even in the presence of the parents. Often she knows nothing of her lover's attachment to her; but even if she does, she must make all possible resistance, which often goes so far, that she suffers herself to be dragged along by the hair; nay, if she persists in not getting up, and in refusing to go quiely, she receives some hearty boxes on the ear. When she at length arrives in the house of the lover, she sits desponding with dishevelled hair, and seizes the first opportunity to run away again. She is fetched back, runs away again, and is again fetched back. If her repugnance is only feigned, she laments, perhaps, for a day or two; but then she yields. If, on the other hand, she dislikes the suitor, she continues to run away, till he either ceases to go after her, or, if he is desperately in love, really employs constraint. In ancient time, the suitor, in such cases, used to cut a few slits in the soles of the feet of the obstinate girl, and was then pretty certain that she would yield, before she was able to walk again. At present, indeed, this rough manner of obtaining a girl's affection is no longer in use; but I know, that, even in my time, a suitor threatened his mistress, who repeatedly ran away from him, with this punishment for her obstinacy. If the girl really dislikes the marriage, for some reason or other, and if she cannot avoid it, in this distress, she cuts off her long hair, and seeks a retreat among the rocks: but by this, she renounces marriage for the future; it must not, therefore, be wondered at, that this step is seldom resorted to. When the troublesome days of courtship are over, and the girl has become a wife, she takes the place of mistress of the house on the bench, provides every thing for her husband, and superintends the household; but if her husband's mother is still living, the latter manages the household, and the wife is, so far, only a maid.

Such a violent kind of courtship cannot be allowed among the baptized Greenlanders; they, therefore, leave the business to the Clergyman, and the way of proceeding is generally as follows. The suitor comes to the Clergyman, and says, "I have a mind to take a wife." "Whom?" He names her. "Have you spoken with her?" Sometimes the suitor answers "Yes, she is not unwilling; but you know how people are." Often he answers, "No!" "Why not?" "That is so difficult; the girls are so shy. Do you speak to her." In this case, the Clergyman sends for the girl; she comes, and after some indifferent questions, he begins his suit as follows. "It will soon be time that you should marry." "I will not marry." "That is a pity: I have a suitor for you." "Whom?" The Clergyman names him. "He is good for nothing; I will not have him." Then the Clergyman enumerates all his good qualities: "He is young, a good and successful fisherman, sits upright in his Kajak, throws his dart with skill and strength, and, what is the most important, he has a good disposition, and loves you." She listens very attentively; her looks betray her approbation; yet she still answers, "I will not marry; I will not have him." "Well, I will not constrain you; I shall easily find a wife for this active young fellow." The clergyman now says no more, as if he considered her "No" as coming from the heart. At last she says softly, with a sigh, or with tears in her eyes, "As you will, Priest." "No!" as you will: I will not persuade you any farther." Now comes a profound sigh, "Yes;" and the affair is settled. Meantime, the suitor awaits his fate. He is sent for, and made acquainted with his good fortune; but told, at the same time, how difficult it was to prevail upon his bride. The wedding day is fixed, of which the girl is already informed. When it arrives, the bridegroom, in his finest clothes, appears with his train, in the house of the clergyman. He advances, with becoming seriousness, to the altar; the clergyman is obliged to take her by the hand, and show her the place where she is to stand. She, indeed, takes her place, but turns away from the bridegroom, that the clergyman is often obliged to turn her a little, so that, when he puts the questions from the book, he can lay her hand in that of the bridegroom. This giving her hand, and the 'yes,' which she must pronounce before all the company, is the most difficult part to her. Generally, she answers only with her eyes, and this, reasonably, passes for a full and sufficient 'yes.' The young couple now go to the house of the bridegroom; he cheerful, she, as it seems, unmoved and cold. Soon after, the clergyman sends them a bushel of peeled barley, or peas, and some stockfish, with his compliments, desiring them to entertain themselves and their friends. Soon the kettles are hung over the lamps; the guests are called; they chat together, and enjoy their little repast with cheerfulness. The bride sometimes suffers herself to be persuaded to taste a little bit, but extremely seldom to lie down, in the evening, in the nuptial bed. However, she never runs away, as the heathen brides do; accustoms herself very well, in a few days, to be a wife; and her former talkativeness and cheerfulness return. If she, as a girl, has observed all this, and the parents have not shown themselves inclined to consent to the match, every one has done his part: she has preserved her honour, and nothing can be said to the disadvantage of the parents.

The Reader will observe, that the clergyman takes a part in the marriage concerns of the baptized Greenlanders, only to prevent the before described manner of courtship, which is so contrary to morality and Christian propriety. He opposes this, without pretending to a right to interfere farther. The suitor, indeed, gives him the commission, the consequences of which are, order and marriage. Long before my time this was the custom in Disco Bay; but I will not affirm that it is the custom all over the country.

Chapter VI.

The Baptism of a Catechumen.

I had once among my Catechumens, at Christianshaab, an elderly widow, who had fled from the southern part of the country, because she was accused, by her neighbours there, of being an Illiseetsok (that is, a wicked sorceress), and her life was, therefore, in danger. Some years before, the wicked wretch who accused her, had been received by her in her house, and she had given him the use of her tent and women's boat, on the condition that he should keep them both in order with skins. For some time he punctually fulfilled this condition but afterwards he conceived a wish to possess them himself. He was pretty sure of obtaining this wish, if he accused her of witchcraft: no sooner thought than done; the innocent, forlorn widow, who was informed of it in time, was forced, in order to save her life, to fly secretly with a sick child, eight or nine years of age, and to abandon her property. She found an asylum, for the present, in the dwelling of a married colonist, near Christianshaab; and as I came there soon after, she applied to me to receive instruction: she received it accordingly, and showed both good-will and capacity. Towards winter I learned her unhappy condition; spoke with her upon it; and promised to protect her as far as lay in my power.

Time passed away, the summer approached, and the baptism of the Catechumens was at hand. After I had performed this solemnity at home, at Claushavn, I went, the week before Whitsuntide, to Christianshaab, in order to go over, daily, the truths of religion with those Catechumens whom, on account of their knowledge and conduct, I thought worthy of baptism. Among these Catechumens was the widow of whom I have spoken. "Will you baptize her?" said the merchant, when I returned from the last examination. I replied, "Yes; she has the necessary knowledge, and expresses a desire for baptism." "I advise you not to baptize her," continued he, "for the Greenlanders who live farther to the south intend to kill her! It would really be very bad if they began to kill baptized persons as witches!" "Should I then," replied I, "expose her to the fury of her persecutors, or rather deliver her up to it, by refusing her baptism? No; that would be a sin. I will baptize her with several others, and thereby lay upon you and your people an obligation more, to defend the life of an innocent person, who is become your fellow Christian." "Neither I nor the people can take upon us to defend her," said he; "we are often absent: her assassins (they lived about a mile from the colony) may watch their opportunity; and, even if we were at home, we should not expose ourselves to the fury of the Greenlanders, for they have resolved upon her death." "Then I will take her with me," replied I, "when I return; and, till then, she may surely be in safety here."

The morning came; it was Whit-Monday. Engaged in reading, I regarded nothing that was passing; till, at length, the cry of "The murderers come! they land!" called my attention.

This visit was, at this moment, as unexpected as it was disagreeable. I collected myself, however, and remained faithful to my purpose, as well to defend the innocent widow, as to baptize her. Two of these men came immediately to the colony, and asked for the priest: they were shown my room, and entered abruptly. After some indifferent discourse, one of them, mentioning her name, said, "Will you baptize her?" "Yes," I replied. "She is good for nothing I," said he; "she is an Illiseetsok." "It is your Angekok," said I, "who accuses her; but he is a liar. I know that you intend to murder her, either now or in the sequel; but I take her under my protection, because she has done no evil; and, when she has become a believer, the Danes and the baptized Greenlanders shall also defend her." They withdrew without replying.

Meantime, the hour of divine service was come, and I sent for the Greenlanders; but, at the same time, begged some sailors to accompany the poor widow, who was probably afraid. The murderers, ten or twelve in number, stood on the place over which she had to pass, but did not attempt to attack her, as they saw that she was not without defenders. She entered the room trembling. "Thou art afraid," said I; "but dost thou not believe, then, that the great God whom thou acknowledgest is more mighty than thy persecutors? Place thy trust in him, and be of good courage." After the sermon, she, as well as the others, rehearsed her belief, and was baptized. Copious tears betrayed her feelings; they were drawn from her by joy, fear, and hope. When divine service was concluded, I said to her, "Now you belong to God, and to us. Thank him, and prove always, by your conduct, that you are a believer." Her persecutors were not yet gone; I, therefore, shut her up in my room while the people were attending divine service, and had her guarded the rest of the day.

The following day, I departed to return home; my wife, who had accompanied me on this journey, the widow, and, her daughter, besides the steersman, and four women to row, were on board. When we had got to a considerable distance from the colony, we perceived several Kajaks, but had not the smallest idea of their being the murderers of yesterday, till they got nearer. The widow recognized them first, and exclaiming, "There they are!" threw herself, with her face downwards, on the bottom of the boat. Her persecutors had heard that I would take her with me, and had, therefore, gone northward, my way, instead of southward, which was their own way home. They rowed rapidly towards us, threw their darts, to show their strength and dexterity in hitting a mark, and, at last, laid one arm on the edge of my boat. Then, certainly, courage was necessary, and it was given me. After some insignificant questions, one of them said, "What woman is that lying there?" "She whom you want to kill," replied I, with firmness; "She is a believer: I take her under my protection, and I shall find means to protect her." They turned pale, and were silent. At last, one of them cried, "That is the same to us." They then suddenly tacked about to the creek, where their tents were set up. We were now so far delivered, and the poor woman began to breathe more freely. Whether it was the eagerness of my women who rowed, to lose sight as soon as possible of these infuriated men, or whatever might be the cause, one of the oars broke; we could not go on well, and we had nothing to repair the oar. We had no means left, but to row into the bay, to the widow's enemies. This was, indeed, extremely hazardous, but, as it could not be otherwise, I resolved upon it, confiding in God, and my good cause. We rowed into the creek, and, at last, landed in the midst of these men, who were all assembled on the shore. I took the broken oar in my hand, went on shore, and said, "Who will repair this oar? I will pay him well." One of them immediately took the oar, and began to repair it. "Akakakn," [13] said some of them to each other, "he is not afraid." They now invited us to their tents (my wife had now come on shore); but I could not accept the invitation, for then, perhaps, it would have been all over with the widow. I, however, conversed with them, till the oar, after we had waited one livelong hour, was repaired. They were content with what I paid: we put from the shore, parted as friends, and reached home in the middle of the night. The widow was now in safety. I placed her and her daughter with a family, who had room to spare. She lived two or three years without suffering want, and died in peace.

Chapter VII.

Some Journies.

I. TO CHRISTIANSHAAB.

I had to make so many journies thither, and many of them so dangerous, that I might very easily fill some sheets with them. About Christmas, I went there by land, and rolled down several times from the summit of high rocks to the foot of them [14]. I travelled on ice which was so thin, that it could scarcely bear the weight of four dogs. I travelled by water, when storms were rising, and often when quantities of drift ice were floating about, which cut holes in my women's boat. But three of these journeys seem to me to be peculiarly dangerous, and worth relating.

I generally went to Christianshaab the day before Easter, as well on account of the Danes, who lived there, as to examine the Catechumens. This time, the sea was open, though full of floating ice. Some sailors, who had been at Claushavn, on commercial business, resolved to accompany me; but when the day for our departure came, they were afraid of the ice, and remained behind. I set off early with a steersman, six women to row, and a Greenlander in his Kajak. With much difficulty and labour, we rowed three miles through the ice, by twelve o'clock. We were saying, that the mile which we had still to go, was not so dangerous, when the steersman suddenly exclaimed, "Look there, up to the rock, Priest! A dreadful storm is rising, which will soon overtake us." I saw it, and answered, "We can scarcely proceed, the resistance is too great; let us put back: we shall find some place in the neighbourhood, where we can stop till the storm is over." We tacked about, but while we were doing so, the storm was already come up, and would, certainly, have overset our boat, had not the Greenlander, with his Kajak, laid himself to windward, and manoeuvred in so masterly a manner against the mighty waves. He let them pass over him, by which they lost some thing of their violence, before they reached us. The boat, however, laboured violently, by which some knees were broken, which made it unsteady. There was not much appearance of our being saved. The women lost their courage, and would not work any longer. "Row!" I cried, and took an oar, "or we shall be drowned!" "We shall be drowned notwithstanding," answered they: "it avails nothing." I encouraged them by words and by my own example, rowed with all my might, and said, "We must do what we can for our safety, and we shall be saved." They now took up their oars again; but the storm continued, our boat became weaker and weaker, and, in truth, our hopes also. After we had laboured for about an hour, with infinite exertions, and had been in the utmost danger of our lives, kind Providence conducted us into a little bay, where the land protected us against the violence of the waves. Here, we found ourselves saved, and thanked God. It cost us some trouble, indeed, to get the boat up over the crust of ice, but we effected it. We turned it upside down, laid ourselves under it upon the snow, and spoke of the danger which we had escaped. The Kajak rower was not a little proud of his exploits and he had reason to be so, for he contributed the most to our deliverance. Some refreshment would now have been welcome, but this was not to be thought of. I had, indeed, two of the biscuits, called Skonsogne, which my wife had made me take when I left home; but what was that among so many?

A part of the afternoon was already gone, when the weather became more calm. "Tomorrow is Easter Sunday," said I to my Greenlanders: "I must go forward by land, or else back." "You joke, Priest," answered my steersman, quickly. "No," answered I. "I am quite serious." "You cannot go forwards," said he; "I have no knowledge of any way. The rocks are terrible, and the way back is so long, you cannot accomplish it." "Let us see," said I; "follow me!" At last I prevailed on my steersman and two women, and set out. As long as it was daylight, we went on well, though the snow was deep; but when night came on, we were unable to distinguish rocks and vallies from each other. We fell into heaps of snow, helped each other up, fell again, and again got up, but became more and more fatigued, and faint. After we had proceeded for some hours, my Greenlander said, "We have missed our way; I no longer hear the sea roar." I listened, and was also unable to hear it. "We must go westward," said I; " the wind has not changed." We did so, and, by extraordinary exertion, came in about two hours nearer to the strand, and soon after to a plain, which was inclosed, on both sides, by high rocks. I thought I recollected this plain, walked up and down on the beach, and found that I really recognised it, having been there the preceding autumn. "We are in Sandbay," said I to my companions when I returned to them, "and are now not far from home." "It is a mile," said my Greenlander, if we go the right way; but we should have scarcely half a mile, if you could clamber up that rock." "Wait a little," said I, and divided my two biscuits among us four. We eat them, drank or swallowed some snow, and felt ourselves a litle refreshed. "Now, up the rock!" I cried. "At the top it is perpendicular," replied my Greenlander; "if your foot slips, you fall into the sea, and no one can save you." "We will try," said I; and now we began, with the little strength we had left, to clamber up. We walked and crawled, but still advanced, however, till we reached the abovementioned steep place. "Now, take care, Priest! don't slip." "Help me," said my Greenlander, "and I will help you when I have got up." He began to climb, and, by the assistance of the women who helped him, got up happily. "Wait a little," said he; "I must rest myself:" but soon after he laid himself on his belly, stretched himself out as far as possible over the steep rock, and said, "Come! I will take hold of you." One of the women clambered up, I helped her, he took her hand, and pulled her up. Now, it was my turn. Both those who were up, and she who was behind, exerted their strength for me: I climbed, my knees tottered; I was near falling, and, consequently, perishing, when I got hold of the out-stretched hand of the Greenlander. By this, and the help of the woman who was behind, I got up [15] safe. "That was good! that was good!" cried my companions. "Yes," said I, "that was good. God be praised. But now, help her who is behind." That they did faithfully; both took her hand, and we were all saved, but so exhausted, that we were obliged to sit down, and rest, ten times during the quarter of a mile which we had still to go.

At length, we reached the colony, on Easter Sunday, at four o'clock in the morning, so exhausted that I fell over the threshold of the kitchen door, and my companions stumbled. I knocked at the door of the chamber, and pronounced my name: my wife was awake, and lay praying to God for my safety; for all the Danes and Greenlanders at Claushavn said, the day before, while the storm raged, that it was impossible we should be saved if we were at sea, but they hoped we might have arrived at Claushavn, before it broke out. While my wife got up, and opened the door, I went to the chamber of my man servant, to wake him, and to tell him to make a fire in the kitchen. He had gone to sleep with the idea that we were all drowned. When I awoke him, and he, still half asleep, recognized my voice, he thought it was my ghost, crossed himself, and said, "God, be merciful to his soul! He was a good man!" "It is myself," said I; "we are saved." Now, he became thoroughly awake, and thanked God from the bottom of his soul [16]. Meantime, my wife had opened the door of the room, and fell upon my neck, with tears of joy. "God then has restored him to me," was all that she could pronounce. Yes! we were restored to each other. After she had become a little calmer, we felt with grateful joy the miraculous deliverance which God had vouchsafed me. But now it was necessary to think of some refreshments for me and my companions; and these were not so easily to be obtained. The fast time had set in [17]; every thing that custom had rendered necessary, wine, brandy, coffee, tea, sugar, &c, was wanting. My wife, therefore, warmed a pot of good beer, with a slice of bread, and some butter. In the condition in which we were, this was, perhaps, the best thing we could have had. We ate

Skonrogn with butter, drank warm beer, and found ourselves refreshed. My Greenlanders went home quite cheerful. I threw myself on the bed for a few hours, and performed divine service at the usual time. Though I had been ill before this journey, it had no bad consequences, except a little pain. At the news of my return, my good Greenlanders came early in the morning to my wife, to inquire after me, and expressed their joy at my safety. My boat, which the Kajak-rower had patched up a little, arrived in the afternoon much damaged. The people were well, but excessively hungry: they had need of refreshment, and received it accordingly.

II. ANOTHER JOURNEY TO CHRISTIANSHAAB.

About twenty or thirty paces from my house there flowed a small stream, with excellent water: it came from the mountains high up the country, formed two fresh-water lakes; and afterwards emptied itself into the sea. In winter it froze over but in spring it broke forth with violence from its sources. If care had not been taken to dig channels to direct its course, it took a wrong direction, and not only overflowed the spot on which my house stood, but even threatened the house itself. This was particularly the case one spring. On the 24th of May I was told that we might expect the stream. My people had, indeed, already done something to guide its course, but not enough. In the forenoon it had already spread over the place, and approached the colony. I had resolved to set out, in the afternoon, on business, to Christianshaab; and had, therefore, ordered the sledge to be ready at two o'clock. The forenoon was employed in instructing the young people but, when it was time for them to go home, the way was intercepted; the swollen stream was already above the threshold of the house, and flowed through my little garden. The children were obliged to get over an out-house, by means of a ladder, in order to reach home, and this was scarcely possible. I wished to dine before I set out: dinner was served up, and we ate; but as my wife was going into the kitchen, and opened the door, it was torn out of her hand, and the water rushed into the room. We were at a loss what to do. There was every appearance that the house might be broken through; and I was to depart. My old Catechist had been already thrown down by the water in the kitchen; and with us in the room all was afloat. My wife and my son could not remain behind; I should else have been tormented by anxious suspense respecting their fate in my absence. At last we set out a great table, put chairs upon it, and endeavoured to save our beds by laying them upon the chairs. We drew the drawers from the wardrobes, and piled them up in the same manner. We wanted now only a napkin, with bread and butter, for a few days, and we were ready. I prevailed upon the Catechist to accompany us; and now we escaped out of the kitchen window, which went out on one side, where the water was not so deep, because the ground was higher. But now we had to walk a pretty considerable distance over the ice [18]; my wife in order to take up her abode in a Greenland house, and I to get to my sledge. But the ice was extremely brittle, hardly any thing but foam, and still more dangerous on account of the stream, which rushed furiously along; and yet we had to go over this very place! Resolved to share the same fate, we took our little son, two years old, between us: the Catechist accompanied us, and we reached, almost without hoping it, our destination for the present. My wife had never yet passed a night in a Greenlander's house, and could not prevail upon herself to sleep upon the bench, among all the naked people. With her back against the wall, and her little boy upon her lap, she held it out for three nights and three days. On the fourth day the stream had returned into its own bed: it was still rapid and furious, but not so broad but that she could attempt to pass it, supported by two Greenlanders, upon a board laid across; and she got home safe. I will say nothing of the destruction in our house and around it. My wife did every thing to put it, in some measure, in an habitable state before my return.

As soon as I had placed her in security, in a Greenlander's house, on the beforementioned 24th of May, I set out upon my journey. The ice was very brittle; not like that upon which we are used to venture at the beginning of winter, but like that which the stream and sun daily undermine and melt away. After we had proceeded two miles, we met with an opening so long that we could not go round it, and so broad that we could not get over, except by a successful jump. My Greenlander said, "We shall not get over unless we take a run before we leap; and then it is a question whether the ice on the other side is strong enough to bear us." We had each of us a tuk [19]. My companion took a run, with his pole in his hand, and got happily over. I also took a run, aimed at the same spot as he, to obtain firm footing, and reached it; but by his weight the ice had already so far burst, that, when mine was added to it, it broke under me, and I fell up to the arms in the cleft. In this situation I should certainly have got under the ice, and have been irrecoverably lost, had not my pole, which as I fell came across the cleft, supported me. I had sunk too deep to be able to help myself up; and my Greenlander did not like to take hold of me, as the circumstances required. "How shall I help you up, Priest?" said he. "Dare I take you by the hair and one arm; for you must not let go of the pole?" "Take hold of me where you think best," answered I; "but as soon as possible, for I grow every moment heavier." Now he quickly took me by the hair and the left arm, but it was necessary for him to be very cautious, that the ice might not break while he was helping me, and thus both of us perish. He pulled me up so far that I could help myself: I, of course, did this more and more in proportion as I was able, and, at last, got out happily, but was wet through. In this condition, I had still two miles to travel [20]. The wind blew cold from the north, and I was, indeed, not warm. However, we got to the end of our journey. On my arrival at Christianshaab, I immediately changed my clothes and linen. The merchant then regaled me with coffee, a good repast, and afterwards with excellent punch, which warmed me thoroughly. I slept well, got up in good health and spirits, and thanked God. When the business which occasioned my journey was finished, I returned home by water. My simple dwelling looked miserably, and yet it had been repaired as far as the time had allowed. My little garden was entirely ruined. My wife and son were in good health, and my Greenlanders were well; everything, therefore, was well.

III. A JOURNEY TO JACOBSHAVN.

I was indisposed, and resolved to go in the Christmas holidays to Jacobshavn, to get my-self blooded by the merchant there: he was the only person, for some miles round, who could perform this operation; but the season was unfavourable; the 20th of December, there was no daylight; so near the equinox; the sea was stormy; the ice unsafe; and the icebergs, which were raised from the bottom by the high sea, extremely deceitful. However, I set out; necessity commanded; and a Greenlander had told me, the day before, that it was possible to go over the ice in the Isefjord. Our party was in two sledges. We travelled half a mile by land, without any accident; but when we had got some part of the way over the bay, the ice grew so thin, that we were obliged to take all the dogs except four from the sledges: we should not have been able to do even this, any more than to turn, had not a piece of old ice given us an opportunity to halt and unharness the dogs. We now continued our journey. At the distance of a musket shot to our left there was open sea, and on our right some Greenlanders were sitting at the foot of the neighbouring icebergs, to shoot seals. Far up the bay, icebergs were falling together with a dreadful crash. At last, after many dangers, we reached the opposite coast. The way to the colony passed over a pretty high rock; we ascended it; looked back; and on the spot over which we had just driven in our sledges, there was no ice now to be seen! We thanked God for our escape, drove on, and reached the colony about eight o'clock in the evening, just as the merchant and the clergyman had sat down to supper.

They had, indeed, heard the barking of strange dogs, but they could not possibly imagine that an European had ventured over the bay at this season, and did not mind it. I entered; and, as I perceived that I was not recognized, I seated myself on a bench near the door. The conversation was respecting me. The merchant turned to me, whom he took for a Greenlander, and asked me, with kindness, whether I had heard any thing today of the clergyman at Claushavn? "I have seen him to-day." "Seen him!" he exclaimed; "you lie!" "No!" said I, and stepped forwards. My arrival, at this time, astonished them; but, at the same time, they were happy to see me alive. Now they made me relate the circumstances of my journey over and over again. "My business," said I, "among other things, is to ask you to bleed me to-morrow." "Very willingly," said he, "if necessity requires it; but it is the equinox, and this season is not considered favourable." The day came and went, without my resolving on any thing: the next day came; but whether it was the change of place, company, or conversation, or whatever it might be, my spirits were more cheerful, my blood cooler, and, as I was advised, I deferred, to another time, the bleeding for which I had come with such imminent danger.

Now I was to return home again, as the holidays were at hand. But how? No Dane would venture, at this season, to go in a vessel out of the Isefjord (only the Greenlander in his Kajak ventures upon it) and in the bay itself, and between the rocks, it was extremely dangerous, though it was said, that, half a mile above the place where I had passed, it was still possible to get over the ice. I resolved, however, to return home, though my friends dissuaded me, and my good wife wrote to me by a Kajak, that the old Catechist would attend to the divine service for the Greenlanders, and would read to the two Danes there, a printed sermon; so that nothing should be neglected, and that I should, by all means, remain where I was.

On the 23d of December, in the morning, I set out on my return: my friends accompanied me for some time; but, when the road began to be difficult, we took leave of each other, as their accompanying me any farther would only have detained me. After great exertions, and many dangers, we came to an iceberg, which, except for the space of two fathoms, was surrounded with open water. We could not pass over this water, nor was there any possibility of passing any where else; we were, therefore, obliged to resolve on climbing over the iceberg, which was not high, and seemed to be sound. A hazardous undertaking! However, we got over the iceberg happily, called our dogs, which swam over to us; and, at last, reached our shore. But the ice was everywhere broken; we could not land; and there was every appearance of our being obliged to remain where we were. For some hours we drove and walked backwards and forwards, till, at last, we found, in a little creek, a narrow slip of ice fast to the land, over which we hastened, and got on shore. But my Greenlanders had never been so far up the country: they knew neither rocks nor vallies; all they knew was, that we must travel towards the south-west, in order, if possible, to reach home. The evening was at hand, and, with that, the darkness. We did not know how long the way was which we had still before us. However, we had escaped the danger of the bay, and drove on full of hope; but, after we had travelled about an hour, one of our sledges, in descending a rock, struck against a large stone: the thong that fastened the dogs to the pole broke; and the dogs ran away, finding themselves free. This impeded our progress, for we were obliged to give the Greenlander a place in our sledge, and allow him to fasten his behind ours. The dogs reached home long before us, and were, as usual, received by the other dog's in the place with noise and barking. This made the Greenlanders come out of their houses; and, as they knew the dogs were still wet, and their coats full of icicles, it was generally believed that we had perished. In anxious expectation, and almost without hope, my wife and the others went about; when the dogs of the colony again began to bark, and thus announced our arrival. The joy of my wife was not to be described. The sudden transition from grief to joy had such an effect on my old Catechist, whose son was my driver, that his scurvy seized him, and held him so fast to the earth, that he could not stir from the spot: I went up to him, and saluted him. To show him that we were not so fatigued as to be unable to be cheerful, I said, "Are we not active people?" "Yes," said he, "so active, that you will one day perish, to the sorrow of us all."

Chapter VIII.

Some Particulars of our Trade with the Greenlanders.

The navigation to Greenland, as well as the trade with the inhabitants, was carried on, some years ago, for the account of the king, who, probably, seldom gained by any trade; but, in general, it has been carried on by a company under the direction of a board [21]. The uninitiated could only guess at the profits, which, in the manner that the trade was managed, must have been considerable. A certain price or tariff was feed for the goods which were sent thither, and, at the same time, it was fixed what payment the Greenlanders should receive for the articles which they disposed of. The goods sent there, consisted, among other things, of kerseys, Silesian linen, cottons, silk handkerchiefs, ribands, beads, scraping-knives, and other knives, harpoon irons, kettles, powder, lead, tobacco, and firearms. The Greenlanders sold blubber, seals' skins, foxes' skins, sometimes bears' skins, whale-bone, unicorns' horns [22], eider down, &c. I do not know what the abovementioned Danish goods cost; but, in my time, the tariff for us Europeans was as follows:

Marcs. Schil. Groschen. Pfennig.

1 Ell of kersey 81 .... 2 10 or 10 6

1 Pound of powder ... 2 or 8
1 Pound of lead... 10 or 26
1 Scraping-knife... 18 or 6
1 Harpoon iron... 18 or 3
(without barbs)
1 Do. with barbs... 12 or 3 [23]

A barrel of blubber, when boiled in Copenhagen, might yield about three quarters of a barrel of train oil. When we know that a tub or barrel of blubber was paid for with no more than the value of a rixdollar, that the Danish goods were sold to the Greenlanders at an advanced price, as we have seen above, and also that the barrel of train oil was worth, in those years, from sixteen to eighteen rixdollars (and, therefore, three quarters of a barrel from twelve to thirteen and a half rixdollars), we see, not only what these necessaries cost the Greenlanders, but also what advantages the company derived from them. But of all the goods, none cost them dearer than a rifle gun, which was so indispensable for them, in Disco Bay, where the ice lies fast for many months, and the seals must be shot. I am not certain, but I was told, that each rifle cost the company six or seven rixdollars: and the Greenlanders were obliged to give ten rixdollars, or ten barrels of blubber, which, according to the calculation above, was a great expense for them, and a great advantage to the company. This expense, however, they could bear: nor was the profit unreasonable when we consider the expenses of fitting out the ships, provisioning the colonies, and then the payment of the numerous persons employed in Copenhagen and in Greenland; to say nothing of the risk of trade in such a dangerous sea: but the Greenlanders paid a great deal more for their goods, and this more was too much.

I will explain my meaning more clearly. They gave, for example, not ten tubs of blubber for a rifle gun [24], but even fifteen, and the tub did not contain one barrel only, but one barrel and a half, and was, besides, without a bottom. When they were to measure, the workmen very cunningly contrived to put the tub over a hole, which was to be filled before the blubber reached the bottom of the tub, and, after that, the tub was filled. The Greenlanders knew, indeed, that this was not as it should be. Some were silent, others laughed and said, "Well, it will be full at last," and all remained on the same footing. I do not exaggerate, but affirm that the Greenlanders, in my time, paid for their guns in this manner. Two or three years passed before they could save so much. They seldom received the gun till they had delivered the half, and when they did, there was often a crack in the barrel, or the lock was damaged, and these faults required new expenses before it was serviceable. In short, they gave an immense price for a gun, which was often very indifferent, and this price is often obtained with difficulty, and at the risk of their lives. The company received only ten barrels: the merchants kept the rest without any scruple for themselves; and yet these were not real merchants, but only commercial agents. They risked nothing in the trade. If they only gave an account of the goods sent over to them, and of the quantity of blubber, whalebone, &c.[25], which they purchased for them, and provided themselves with a certificate from the captain, for the goods which they sent home, they were exempt from all loss, even should the ship perish; they ought, therefore, to have been contented with a smaller profit. It was absolutely necessary to allow them some profit; for example, so much percent on the quantity of blubber which they sent home, or premiums when they sent a certain quantity, &c.; for most of them know no other blessing than profit; and, without hope of obtaining this, none of these commercial agents would remain in Greenland, and the trade would stand still. I must be very much mistaken if the company does not gain upon the goods which it receives according to the appointed tariff; but how much more would it gain, would the mother country and the poor Greenlanders gain, if the appointed tariff, both for the Greenland and Danish goods, were followed, and the whole quantity of blubber obtained from the colonies turned to the advantage of the legal trade?

The merchants were very mysterious, even respecting the goods which they sent home to the company; but I know, however, that from the two places where I was Minister, there were shipped, for its account, from one hundred and thirty to two hundred barrels of blubber[26]; nay, one year certainly, three hundred barrels, besides other goods, such as whalebone, skins, &c.

If the Minister, as the representative of the Greenlanders, particularly of those who were baptized, spoke or wrote to the merchant on the injustice of such proceedings, the peace between them was broken, and many unpleasant consequences ensued: if he sent such ac- counts home, he was a quarrelsome man, a man who meddled in things which did not concern him, and effected nothing. The directors of the company trusted their servants, and the missionary college was so convinced of their honesty, that, before we departed, it enjoined us, among other duties, to live upon good terms with the merchants. The favour, which we might expect at our return, in some measure, depended upon it.

My merchant and I always observed outside appearances, and God knows that I had no desire to injure him. At times, indeed, I was obliged to write to him, but without bitterness; and, in our conversations, all such things seemed to be forgotten. At my departure, he wept, and wished fervently that I could and would remain; and, after my return to my own country, the missionary college gave me a complaint, made by him, to answer. It stated, that I had carried on an illicit trade [27] with the Greenlanders. I was convinced that, as an honest man, I ought to contribute my part to set bounds to irregularities, by which so many people were injured, when an opportunity presented itself; and I obtained it in the following manner.

I gave a hint of some of the things which I have mentioned above. I received for answer, "Be so good as to give it in writing." I wrote, but at the same time desired not to be considered as an informer. I wished to see nobody called to account; I only wished that it might be made impossible for those concerned, to act towards the Greenlanders as they had hitherto done. For this purpose, I proposed that legal tubs or barrels should be sent to Greenland, which should have a bottom, but hold a barrel and a quarter, because the merchants, without this excess, would be sufferers; also that the Greenlanders should be publicly informed that they should not suffer their blubber to be measured with any barrels beside these, &c. I have reason to believe, that my proposal was partly followed, particularly as the king sent to Greenland, in the following year, two civil officers, called Inspectors, whose office something resembled that of the bailiffs here in Denmark. It was an important duty for them, to watch over the conduct of the merchants, and to take care that the Greenlanders were not cheated. I hardly need to observe, that I have spoken here of the trade, only as it was carried on in my time, and particularly in Disco Bay.

Chapter IX.

The Wedding.

I have said above that the Minister must interfere in marriage concerns, and also given the reasons for it. There would be, therefore, nothing more to say on the subject, had not the wedding, of which I am going to give an account, been very remarkable, and very near costing me dear.

The son of the Catechist, of mixed race, a

handsome, well made, and active Greenlander, had fallen in love with the handsomest girl in the colony. She was sensible, modest, and domestic; so that his father had no objection to his attachment. The parents who, indeed, perceived his inclination to the girl, allowed him to frequent their house, and thus gave him an opportunity to see and speak to his mistress. Some years passed in this manner; but the constraint to which they were subject in these visits, was, at last, importunate to the lovers, as their passion increased. They sought and met each other in other places, and had frequent secret interviews [28]. The Greenlanders began to speak doubtfully concerning them. As soon as I perceived this, I told his father what I had heard, and proposed to him to let the young people marry. "Very willingly," said he; "I desire their union, the sooner the better." I sent for the father of the girl, and, after a short preface, said, "You know that Peter loves your daughter Louisa: you can have nothing against their marrying, as he is able to provide for a wife, and is a worthy young man." "I want her services myself," said he. "She cannot always serve you," said I; "you have certainly heard what people say; and, as her father cannot allow her reputation to be hurt." "The people lie," said he; "if she shall not have him." "You say that," continued I, "merely to follow the old custom. In our country, parents rejoice to see their daughters well married before they die, but it is your way always to affect opposition. If you die, who shall take care of your daughter, who may, by that time, have become an old maid?" "It is all the same," said he, in a tone of displeasure, and rose to go away; "she shall not have him." "She shall have him," said I; "I dare not allow young people to live a disorderly life." He was silent, and withdrew. The

Catechist, who was so well acquainted with the way of thinking of the Greenlanders, was of opinion that the opposition was of the usual kind, and was of no consequence. I appointed the day for the wedding; for the Minister always fixes the day, and acquaints the parties concerned. I wished to do as much honour to the festival as possible, in order to show the father of the bride-groom how much I valued him as a teacher. I therefore invited the young couple and their parents to dine with us on the wedding-day, ordered the flag to be hoisted, &c.

The day and hour came; the bridegroom appeared with his train, but the bride did not come. I sent a messenger for her; but the messenger came back, and said the father was angry, and would not let the girl go. I was dressed to perform the ceremony: my wife said, therefore, "I will go and fetch her," and went; but she, too, came back without the bride, and said that the father watched her as a miser did his treasure. What was now to be done? The resistance was unusual; for the parents always let their daughters go, even though they appear to be displeased [29]. The dignity of my office would have suffered by yielding, which, in this case, would have been weakness [30]; I, therefore, put on my pelisse, and went myself to fetch the girl. "Do not go there, good Priest!" said a woman to me as I went along: "he is malicious." "You know," said I, "that I desire only what is right, and he must obey me." "We shall see," said she, as I went on. When I entered the house, I saw him sitting on the side bench, next his daughter (she sat, undressed, on the right-hand bench); and besides them some women. "Why do you make so much resistance?" said I. "You know why your daughter must now marry: let her go." "You may take her," answered he, violently, "and make her your concubine; but he shall not have her." "Now you are malicious," said I: "we blame your countrymen who have concubines, and you offer your daughter as such to the priest! Put on your pelisse," said I to the girl, seriously, "and come with me to my house." She hastily threw on her pelisse, and passed by her father, who said nothing, and let her go. I did not observe any change in his countenance; but the women must have remarked it, for they all went out, as I supposed, to accompany the bride. When we were alone, I said to him, "You see that your opposition availed nothing: I have invited you to dinner to-day; come now with me; see your daughter married; and dine with me." He made no answer. "Very well," said I; turned from him, and went to the door of the passage out of the house; but, as I stooped, in order to go down into the passage, I perceived that he was behind me. I immediately stood upright; and, turning round, saw him with his arm lifted, and a large knife in his hand, with which he intended to stab me in the back, as soon as I had got with half my body into the passage, and, therefore, would be incapable of making any resistance. I instantly seized him, and threw him on the ground; but he seized me round the body, and held me so fast, that I fell on the ground with him. In a rage, he endeavoured not only to get loose, but also to give me the meditated blow: he succeeded in neither; but, as he was naked, and I could only hold him fast by the hair, it cost me trouble enough to manage him. "Now I could beat you, use you ill, and you deserve it; but I will not: I must defend my life, of which you so basely attempted to deprive me, but not revenge myself; thus the great Teacher commands." "That is the same to me," replied he, foaming at the mouth. While this was passing, my man came with his sledge near the house, to fetch turf [31]. "Quick! go in! Frederick! the Priest!" and other unconnected words, exclaimed the Greenland women. He came: "Good God, Sir! What is that? What shall I do?" cried he, almost beside himself. "Try to get the knife from him," said I; "take care of it, and of all the others that you can find: till you have done that, I dare not let him go." He took my adversary by the right arm; but, in disarming him, received a severe cut in the finger. At this time, a young Greenlander happened to return from fishing. The women, in their terror, told him what had happened: he immediately left his boat, and came in to us. "Priest," said he, "I will help you. Oh! the villain!" This offer was the more laudable, as the Greenlanders are, in general, averse to hurting each other. "I thank you for your good will," said I; "but now he cannot do much more." These words gave him strength to make some faint attempts to get loose without assistance. At last he said, "Let me go, Priest." I left him under the guard of his countrymen, went away, having first reproved him for his base and unlawful conduct. When I got into the open air, I heard my wife, in the utmost consternation, ask the Greenland women about me, and for the house in which she had just been herself, for one of them had called out, "Come, good lady; Frederick has doubtless stabbed the Priest!" She saw me, and wept for joy.

While all this was passing, the young couple and the attendants had been waiting for me. I came now, and, as soon as I had put my dress in order again, let the ceremony begin with a psalm; but when I was going to advance, in order to speak, the Catechist said to me, in a whisper, "You must not stand just before the window: he knows that you always stand there when you perform the marriage ceremony, and he might be wicked enough to shoot you through the window." I was, therefore, obliged to change my place, and make the young couple change theirs. The ceremony began and finished; and never did a Greenland bride give me such a willing and plain answer as this one. The young couple, the Catechist, and his wife, dined with us (the train, as usual on such occasions, I had entertained in a Greenland house); but, though I tried to encourage them, there prevailed in the company a silence, a fearful presentiment of some misfortune impending over me, which Providence graciously averted. Notwithstanding all the opposition that the father had made, he was soon reconciled to his son-in-law; the marriage was happy. I took my usual walks without apprehension; and he never afterwards tried to injure me.

Chapter X.

Sequel to the preceding Chapter.

It may easily be supposed, that the event related in the preceding Chapter was soon generally known. Since the time of the late Hans Egede, nobody had yet ventured to lay hands upon the Priest, or upon any European. It was spoken of at visits, and, especially, at the fishing places, where so many persons are sometimes assembled. The most, particularly my baptized Greenlanders, considered his conduct as a crime towards their good Priest, as they called me; others smiled, and said, "So, then, there are, at last, people who dare show the Danes that they are not masters here." The Danes in the neighbouring colonies heard the news with astonishment and wrote me word, that, if the account were true, this Greenlander must be publicly whipped; and that, if I desired it, their people should come to inflict the punishment. I thanked them; but, at the same time, assured them that I did not think of taking any revenge; that what had passed would have no farther consequences, &c. However, he no longer frequented our Christian assemblies: I sent to him, but he made an excuse; I went to him, but he always contrived to avoid me.

About a year had passed in this manner, when an epidemic distemper attacked the Greenlanders, and carried many off; so many, indeed, that, at last, the healthy were not sufficient to bury the dead: they then crept with their corpses to me, and left it to my care to do the rest. From morning to evening I went about among all their sick; spoke to them, and gave them the medicine which I judged proper for them. Some became deaf; to these I was obliged to cry every thing aloud: others became delirious; with these I was forced to watch for lucid intervals: all had a most dreadfully offensive breath. Five or six weeks passed before the disorder sensibly diminished: it was, in truth, in many respects, a hard time for a feeling heart [32].

One morning, after I had returned home from paying my first visits to the sick, to take a little breakfast, my Greenlander suddenly entered the door, and stood still. I asked him to sit down: he did so; but was still silent, and cast his eyes on the ground. At last, I broke the silence; and inquired his business. "I wish much to speak to you, Priest," said he; "but I am unworthy, and I suppose you will not help me." "Certainly I will help you," answered I, "if I can: have you anyone sick?" "My only son," replied he, "is very ill." "I spoke to him but yesterday," said I, "and, when I asked him after his health, he told me he was well and hearty." "Yesterday evening," continued he, "he became ill, very ill." This youth, seventeen or eighteen years of age, was well-informed; read and wrote well; promised to become an active fisherman; and was his father's only earthly hope. While I was making myself ready to accompany him, I said to him, "But tell me now, was it really your intention to kill me, or did you merely mean to frighten me?" "It was my intention to kill you," answered he: "if you had not suddenly turned round, and thrown me on the ground, my knife would certainly have put an end to your life. I was malicious; I was mad. Can you forgive me? Will you help me?"- "I have forgiven you," I answered: "our great Master in Heaven forbids us to revenge ourselves on those who injure us and commands us to forgive them, as he forgave his murderers. Now come!" I accompanied him to his house; I fervently prayed to God (why should I conceal it?) that the youth might live. His recovery, thought I, will thoroughly convince the father of my forgiveness; and religion will gain by it. I afterwards visited him every day, as I did my other patients, but he died. This loss, this great affliction, deeply affected the father; but, at the same time, produced a change in him for the better. A few days after the death of his son, he came to me again: "I am greatly afflicted, Priest!" said he; "have you consolation for me?" This confidence, especially from him, gave me infinite pleasure, and I made use of it. From that time, he not only came to divine service on the Sunday, but also to daily prayers, and to the teaching of the catechism. Every week he visited me once or twice; and almost every time one of his questions was, "Priest, have you forgiven me?" I gained him entirely; and he also gave me one proof more of the truth which I so willingly cherish, that, by reasonable and Christian kindness, we can effect much more, with most men, than by severity. Should I have gained this man (I trust, with confidence, that I gained him for heaven), if, by the help of others, I had had him bound to a stake, and chastised?

Chapter XI.

The Child Saved.

Among the heathens, when a mother, who has a child at the breast, dies, and there is no other mother near who can suckle it, the child is generally buried alive with its deceased mother. Thus I once learned, that the heathens, half a mile to the north of me, had laid a child, about a quarter of a year old, with its mother in the grave, but, from a certain degree of feeling, had not wholly stifled it by the stones which they had laid upon the grave. They heard it faintly moan, and so it lived for about a day. This account, the first in its kind since I had come to Greenland, greatly affected me. Some days afterwards, I went to these people, to reprove them for the wrong they had done. They did not deny the deed, but would not have it looked upon as cruelty. "What shall we do, Priest?" said they: "you know that we love our children; but if the mother of the poor little things die while they are at the breast, and no other woman is near, who can take care of them, they must either die of hunger, or cry themselves to death: is it, then, not better that we, out of compassion, give them a quicker death?" In fact, they have no means to support such innocent little creatures but the breast; no milk, no light food. I could of course not approve of their cruel compassion, but told them, that, if such a case should often happen, they should inform me of it; I would then fetch the orphan child, and have it brought up. About a year after this, one of these Greenlanders came to me in a hurry. "Priest," said he, "we have not forgotten your words; M.N.'s wife bore a boy to-day, and died. All the others are absent, as you know; and there is no one to suckle him. Will you take him? if not, we bury him with his mother." I thanked him that he had remembered my words, gave him a little present, and immediately sent my women's boat to fetch the boy, whom they brought me well and hungry. My wife put him to the breast, he satisfied his first hunger, and fell asleep. Meanwhile, I persuaded a Greenland woman, for payment, to give him the necessary attention, for our own son was not yet a quarter of a year old; but he received from my wife his daily nourishment. He grew and throve by it, and began to take notice. His smiles were her reward. I baptized him the following Sunday, and called him after a brother of my wife's, to make him dearer to her. The day before, the father came to me, and asked me whether I would baptize his child. On my answering in the affirmative, he asked permission to be present. He obtained it, under the condition that he would be quiet. He came. Every thing which he saw and heard during divine service, was new and surprising to him; but he was all ear. During the baptismal ceremony, a tear started into his eyes; why? he did not know himself. When divine service was over, I said to him, "Now, your son is my son; nay, more than mine: he now belongs to the great Lord in heaven, who will make him unspeakably happy." "Yes," answered he "you have behaved to him like a father, and your wife is like a real mother; but now I will live with you, and be obedient, and become a believer; I may then see him sometimes?" "Yes," answered I, "daily, if you like." He, in fact, came soon afterwards, with his whole family, often saw his son, and was baptized the following year.

After the custom of the country, the boy was now our son, and, as such, he became daily dearer to us. I often fancied him as the well educated youth, as the enlightened, upright man, as a useful teacher among his countrymen; but a prevailing and mortal epidemic tore him from us at the age of a year and a quarter. We lost him; but he attained a better life.

Chapter XII.

Witchcraft.

One Sunday afternoon, I visited a sick woman, whose indisposition, which was only a cold, was soon removed by a perspiring draught: but while she was in her perspiration, her brother, who was a conjurer, unhappily came to visit her. He saw her perspire, and asked, "How? what is that?" She said she was sick, but that the Priest had given her something to make her perspire, after which she would be well. "No," said he, mysteriously, "that is not the case, you are still sick: a wicked witch has brought it on you." The persons present were attentive, and looked at each other embarrassed. "I will soon discover her," said he; and what was unusual among the baptiied Greenlanders, the husband allowed him to show his art. He did it with the usual formalities, and the result was, that an elderly woman in the place, against whom he, perhaps, had a spite, was, as he pretended, the person who had bewitched her. "Under the bench," cried he, "I see her spirit, which tries to seize you." "Fire! fire!" cried he to the husband and the others: "drive her away! kill her." Immediately they seized their guns, and fired several times at the wicked spirit. At the same time, they howled and cried aloud.

I wondered, indeed, at hearing musket shot

at this time, but could form no conjecture of the cause. A Greenlander now put his head into the door of the room, and cried, "Priest! Priest! come up to the houses! They are mad." I hastened after him to learn something more before I got there; and he told me what I have just related, and also that the woman who was accused of being a witch, was almost dead with terror. My way led me past her door; I went in, and found her in a state like that of a person who, trembling, awaits her death. "Be of good cheer," said I; "they shall do you no harm. God in heaven protects the innocent." I spoke these words with confidence, though I did not know how the people would receive me in their present temper, and what effect my address to them might produce. I entered the house, which was full of the smoke of gunpowder; and the guns which had been discharged, still lay there. All were much confused when they saw me, particularly the master of the house. I was serious, but not angry. "Sit down, Priest," said he, at last, and laid the bear skin in order. I sat down, and shoved aside the fire-arms that lay near me. "What do they here?" said I. "Whence this smell? What is the cause of so many shot?" many questions at once, indeed, but all leading to the same point. The man was silent. "Are you still sick?" said I to the wife: she, too, was silent. "You are no longer sick," said I, firmly: "you only pretend to be so. I know all that has passed here. You," said I to the husband, "have had conjuring tricks performed over your wife: the conjurer has accused Paul's wife of being a witch; you have fired at her spirit, and designed to kill her: you are wicked men." "How do you know that?" said he, abruptly. "I know it," I replied; "and now I tell you, if ever you suffer any conjuring in your house again, you cannot be a believer, and not live among them. Another time I will convince you that you have acted wrong, for now you are not in a condition to regard my words but, if you kill Paul's wife, or suffer her to be killed, you shall be severely punished: she is innocent. I take her under my protection." "I will not kill her," said he, with a suppressed voice, but was in violent agitation. "Where is the conjurer," asked I, " who dare to perform his tricks here, and to corrupt my believers?" I looked around, and perceived him lying under a large skin. I arose, threw the skin off him, and seized him firmly by one shoulder. He sat down. "You are an impostor," said I, "and can do only evil; you do not cure your sister; I have cured her: to-morrow you shall come to me." He did not answer. At last I went away; and, on my return, called on the poor woman, who was still suspended between fear and hope. "No one shall lay hand on you," said I: "trust in God, and be comforted!"-"Thank you, Priest!" answered she, "my soul now begins to live again." The conjurer came to me the next day, as I had desired; but, out of fear he had prevailed on his baptized brother, who had not been present at the conjuration, the preceding evening, to come along with him. The brother came in first, and said, "my brother is with out but he is afraid.""He is afraid," said I, "because he has done evil: he who does good is not afraid." I called him in; and he came very humbly. "I should have good reason to punish you," said I; "but, as you do not know yourself what evil you might do among my believers by your conjurations, I will spare you; but on condition that you never come here again." "I will never come again," answered he; and, as long as I was in the country, he kept his word. "One thing more," added I: "should any one venture to kill Paul's wife, you shall be considered as the perpetrator; and I shall find you, wherever you may be." "She shall not die," he replied. "Well, then, return home; and do not forget what you have promised me."

Chapter XIII.

The Whale found.

The Greenlanders are extremely rejoiced when they have taken a whale, and they have reason to be so, as it affords them great advantages. The men put on their water-proof coats, and the women adorn themselves: the latter tow the animal to the shore, singing; while the former, like ravens, sit upon it, and rip off the skin.

They always sent a Kajak to inform me of such a prize; and, at the same time, invited me and my wife to see it. When we arrived, they received us with songs. "There comes our good Priest," said they, "and his good wife: they will see our whale, and rejoice with us. Come and see!" When we returned home, they sang again: sometimes we accompanied them on shore, at least as near to the land as the animal could swim. The women rowed home, with joyful songs; and the men proceeded seriously to their profitable work.

They had once pierced a whale, pursued him, and cut him in some places, yet he escaped; though they had so wounded him that he afterwards died. He was found, in the winter, about a mile from the colony. I was, as usual, invited to see this prize, and, as I had just to make a journey to the south, on business, I accepted this invitation, and stayed with them several hours. Though the frost was very severe, and the ice thick, there was yet open water round the dead animal, and the Greenlanders were hard at work. Some cut off whalebone, under the water; others blubber. The dogfish regaled themselves, and bit out large pieces of fat with their sharp teeth; only, when they came too near the Greenlanders, the latter pushed them away. They helped me to draw one of them upon the ice, and cut him open: the stomach was full of pieces of whale fat; and the flesh moved long after it was dead. The Greenlanders value this animal but little, as its flesh is not to their taste, and has no blubber; only the liver contains the very finest train oil: they throw it into a cask, and it dissolves entirely into oil; but the Greenlanders do not think it worth their while to catch it for this reason. I jumped upon the dead whale, and walked some steps up and down on a piece of spungy flesh: they told me that it was the tongue. I examined it more closely, and thought how suitable it was to the great jaws and the immense body. It is generally known that the swallow of this animal is no larger than a great tea cup, that it has no teeth [33], and that it lives and fattens on small insects that are found in these waters. I took leave of my Greenlanders, and continued my journey.

On these occasions, their joy makes the Greenlanders very careless. With long knives, like sword blades, they dive under the water to cut off the whalebone: often one stands on the shoulder of the other to keep him under the water, as his water-proof cloak would otherwise cause him to rise. When he who is under the water can no longer hold his breath, he makes a motion with his body, and the man who stands upon his shoulders leaps off. He now thrusts his knife upwards, and rises with a loud roar, which is caused by the air being so long compressed. It was upon such an occasion that a misfortune happened, which was great enough in itself, but which might have had still more melancholy consequences. A Greenlander, who had been under the water, thrust his knife upwards, perhaps with more carelessness than usual, and run it into the body of another, who was rather higher, cutting off the kin. The deceased was the most respectable of my baptized Greenlanders, and his death would certainly have been revenged, if the circumstance had happened among the heathens. To testify his regret, the perpetrator took him on his lap, as they rowed home, and the next day gave to the foster-son of the deceased a new rifle gun, by way of atonement for the grief which he had caused him by his unhappy imprudence. Among others, there came some heathen friends, to console with the widow. These dropt some hints that the murder ought to be revenged; but the widow answered, "That will not bring my husband back again: the murder was not done on purpose, and I am a believer."

The moment I was informed of this unhappy event, I hastened home, in order to prevent any farther misfortune, if there should be reason to fear it. I went immediately to the afflicted widow, who related to me, with tears, the virtues of her husband, and his affection for her [34]. She promised me that she, being a Christian, would never allow any harm to be done to the perpetrator. He lived, however, in constant fear of death, became inactive, and was nowhere at ease, nay, he even begged me to send him to our country, where alone he would be in safety. I was often obliged to assure him that he should not be afraid for his life, as the act was involuntary, and the widow had pardoned him; but, as he was the same man, who had allowed his heathen brother-in-law to perform a conjuration over his sick wife, as I have mentioned above, I represented to him, at the same time, that this uneasiness and anxiety, perhaps, came upon him as an atonement for the distress which he had caused the innocent woman, who was accused as a witch. "Now," I said, "he might feel himself what it was to fear every moment a violent death." "I did wrong," said he; "and now I am afraid." "Yes," said I; "she too was afraid, but you did not regard it. God preserved her, as she was innocent; he will also preserve you, as your action was not voluntary, and you, besides, so sincerely repent it." In this manner, I, by degrees, made him easy but a certain melancholy hung upon him ever after. His former activity returned, but he was more frequent and more serious in his attendance on divine service. In short, this misfortune made a better man of him; for though not vicious, he was before the most indifferent among my baptized Greenlanders.

Chapter XIV.

Some characteristic Features.

Liberty and equality are the property of the Greenlanders. No one assumes any kind of authority over others. Every one is independent, and can do what he thinks fit. Respect is, however, shown to the meritorious, that is, to the active and successful fisherman. His word has always a certain weight in their conferences, and they frequently pay him a kind of voluntary obedience, though without any farther consequences either to him or themselves. Their good disposition, and their natural modesty, prevent this liberty from exceeding the bounds of propriety. Without magistrates, without laws, they live in peace and harmony: you never hear a dispute about property, never a reproach made to him who has unawares done another an injury: the first accuses himself; the latter makes him easy, and says, "it is of no consequence."

The women attend to the household concerns, do their needlework, and chat familiarly together during the day, when the men are from home fishing; and when the latter come home, they relate to each other, as good friends, their success and accidents in their fishery. They eat what the fortune of the day has procured, or what the house affords; and are satisfied, even if their hunger is hardly allayed.

The inhabitants of one place live in mutual friendship, and share their goods with each other. If, for example, a white fish [35] is taken, they prepare an entertainment. It is speedily cut up, and put in the kettles. They invite their neighbours to dinner, and the house is immediately full of guests: they eat, converse, and are merry. If two, three, or more, of these animals are caught on the same day, company must be invited to all, and they must be all eaten up. I was present one evening at the fourth entertainment, and wondered at the appetite with which they devoured this repast. "But," said I, "how can you eat so much at once and you eat as if you were still hungry!" "We can eat a great deal, and we can fast, as it happens," was the answer. "Feel, Priest," said a man, pointing to his belly, "it is now like a stretched drum [36], but soon, perhaps, it may be as lank as an empty bladder." He meant that in a short time he might be unfortunate in the chase. At such entertainments, and whenever they are very successful in fishing, they never neglect to send their portion to the widows and orphans, even before they themselves eat. "The poor," say they, "have no husband, no father, no one to rejoice them with their success in fishing."

They are hospitable to strangers, according to the manner of the country. The visitor remains on the outside till he is invited to enter. When he enters, the master of the house shews him a seat, and understands, on this occasion, how to treat him with due respect. The wife asks for his clothes, to dry them, and then gives him refreshment; but he does not eat immediately at the first invitation, that he may not appear hungry. During and after the repast, they chat till it is time to go to sleep. The inhabitants of the house lay themselves down, one after the other; and the stranger (so decorum requires) last. The Europeans, however, do not observe this rule of politeness, and the natives excuse them from it.

When on my journies to the south, I was obliged to take up my night's lodging among the heathens: I saw them all assembled on the beach at my arrival. Every master of a family invited me; and he, whose invitation was accepted, considered it as an honour. Soon he showed me a seat, which was covered with a piece of clean bear's skin; and the wife took my pelisse. In a short time, I was visited by almost all the men of the place, whom I entertained with accounts of my country, of navigation, of agriculture, of the growth and preparation of corn, &c. When I took out my little box with provisions, the host or hostess used to say, "It is a pity, Priest, that you do not eat our food; you are in other respects like one of us." After a time, I dismissed my visitors, by saying I was sleepy. The host then gave me his own sleeping place, next to his wife [37], who took all possible care of me, and, repeatedly, asked if I was comfortable. I, indeed, answered in the affirmative; but, without being insensible to the honour shown me, I found the bed hard, my sleep short, and my ribs sore, though I used them all alike. My provision-box was the pillow, my short pelisse the quilt, the boards of the bench, covered with seals' skins, the bed: but I accustomed myself to this; as one gets accustomed to every thing, and, at last, slept very well on such a bed. The reader must not, however, think that the man so entirely trusts his wife to others: no, he merely resigned to me his place as husband, as the most honourable, and laid himself down on the other side of her, where the children usually sleep. When I took leave, I always gave them a little present of bread and tobacco; and they were so well satisfied with it, that they invited me to visit them on my return.

They abhor theft, particularly among each other; they, therefore, do not shut up their things, but put them carelessly and openly, not only every where about the house, but even on the flat roof of the house; and no stranger ventures to touch them, or take any part away. Formerly, they were not so scrupulous, when they could find an opportunity to pilfer any thing from a Dane; but this is no longer the case, unless it be done by a heathen from some distant part, and even that is now rare.

As they are well made, fleshy, and full of blood, the sexual passion develops itself early;

and the young men, therefore, look out for a wife as soon as they are able to maintain one, but not before. Youthful excesses are, however, disapproved among them, and are very seldom heard of. In the whole time of my residence in the country, only one girl had become pregnant by her lover before marriage; but she had to pay dear enough for her imprudence. But, properly, this temperance is found only between the natives of both sexes: towards the Danes, on the contrary, the girls are even forward: they love to dress and show themselves; and even interpret a smile to their advantage. That they do not understand each other's language, is no great obstacle to them; for, if a Dane has learnt the words (which are, generally, the first that he learns after his arrival) "I love you;" and if he, at the same time, lays his hand on his heart, the girl feels herself flattered, and happy in his love [38]. Vanity, by which so many have fallen, has, doubtless, more share than inclination in this preference given to the Danes; for a girl who marries a sailor can lead a more easy life, live better, dress better, be more respected, keep maid servants, and eat at pleasure, sometimes Danish, sometimes Greenland food. How seducing is all this, even when no personal preference is given! Neither the heathens nor the Christians marry their relations; not even in a remote degree: they consider it as improper, and carefully avoid it; nay, they think with so much delicacy on this subject, that, when a man educates a charge child among his own, it is considered as their brother or sister; and I am not acquainted with a single instance, of children thus brought up together having married each other.

On some occasions, the Greenlanders show a

want of courage, nay, even cowardice. If they are sensibly offended or ill treated, or when they want to kill a witch, they set little value upon their lives; otherwise, an active Dane can make many of them run away. Sometimes they make up for this cowardice by cunning, and secretly take away the life of their enemy, whom they are afraid to attack openly. If the murder afterwards becomes known, it is looked upon by every body with indifference, only the nearest relations of the deceased revenge it in time, if an opportunity offers. They are capable of bearing fatigue and inconvenience without regarding them; and they show courage and presence of mind in danger. Without desponding, they endeavour to preserve their lives as long as possible; but are, at the same time, indifferent to death, when it cannot be avoided.

The merchant at Christianshaab had once taken a journey, for some miles, in the company of a Greenlander. While they were stopping at the place they had gone to, a storm arose from the south-east [39]. They, therefore, hastily set out to return home; but, when they had got about half way, the ice had broke, and drove, in large flakes, from the coast to which they were going. They drove backwards and forwards, but did not advance much. The flakes of ice broke more and more to pieces; and there was every appearance that they would be obliged to abandon their sledges, and try to save their lives, as long as possible, by jumping from one piece to another. "Merchant," said the Greenlander, quite composed, "you cannot jump as I can; and it does not appear that I can help you: perhaps I may save my life; you hardly will. Hear! you have a pencil and paper in your book; tear a piece out, and write here, upon my back (he stooped down as he said this), that you were drowned; otherwise your people might believe, when I come on shore, that I have killed you." The merchant, it may be supposed, had no mind to do this; but begged the Greenlander, for God's sake, not to forsake him. "I will not forsake you," answered the Greenlander; "but you may be drowned in taking a leap, when I can be saved by it. However, if you die, I can die also; and then nobody can find fault." This conversation lasted but for a few minutes. At last, after much labour and danger, both saved their lives, and were rejoiced; but the Merchant could not forget the coolness with which the Greenlander had persuaded him to write that he was drowned; and the other joked with him about it: "That was droll," said he; "the Merchant would not write! You were afraid, Merchant!"

The Greenlanders are much too careless about the future; and, therefore, do not properly prepare for the possible case, that their fishery may be unsuccessful. In summer, they, indeed, provide themselves with some bags of dried herrings, and dried seal's flesh; but, if their fishery is unsuccessful for some time, and they are obliged daily to take from this little store, it is soon consumed, and they are threatened with want. In severe winters, they are frequently obliged to suffer hunger, in a greater or less degree; but still they do not, upon the whole, become more prudent. They always hope for future success; and, in the literal sense of the expression, let every day bear its own burden.

Chapter XV.

The Severe Winter.

Every winter, in Greenland, is severe; but they are not all equally so. The Danes have observed, that, if the winter in Denmark has been severe, that in Greenland was, in its kind, more mild, and vice versa. During my stay there, one winter was distinguished by its severity. The ice lay, for many months, fast in the gulph, for ten miles, and to the island Disco, which was seldom the case. The seals retired so far, that the Greenlanders, with all their rowing, and with the greatest activity, could not procure the necessary food for themselves and families. Their winter provisions were soon consumed, want, and, soon after, real famine, was at hand. The heathens, half a mile to the north of my place of abode, were, like the other Greenlanders, obliged to slaughter their dogs, though they are as indispensable to them as horses to us; not to say that they never eat dog's flesh. When these were gone, they tore the old hard skins from the walls, put them in soak, and attempted to eat them. This they could, indeed, do, because the Greenlanders have excellent teeth: though weak. Many died for want. I could not and durst not see this want, among my baptized Greenlanders and Catechumens, without helping them, as far as possible. I first distributed my stock of meat and bacon, which I bought every autumn for widows who had little children; and, when this was gone, I had, two days in the week, some groats and peas boiled in my brewing copper, and distributed. My wife filled the dishes of the hungry; and, at the same time, divided some stockfish. They received these gifts thankfully, and with joy. "You bad [40] Danes," said they once, "have provisions so far from your own home, and even for us, who suffer want in our own country." This distribution continued long, and, at last, brought me into debt [41]; but I had also the pleasure, that my Greenlanders had strength to work when the fishery began; while, on the contrary, the heathens were so weakened or sick, that they could not, for a long time, make use of the fishery. With what pleasure would I have relieved their wants also! Several received help, for a moment; but it was impossible to relieve them all.

Chapter XVI.

The Mode of Instruction.

The opinion, that nations who live in a high northern latitude are more indolent, and more dull of conception, seems, to me, not applicable to the Greenlanders. That they are ignorant in things of which they have never heard, cannot be brought as a proof against them, if it can be shewn that they are not only ingenious, and inventive in things which relate to their daily life, and employment, but also that they soon understand instruction which is given them. They have a quick comprehension, a retentive memory, and readily imbibe those religious truths which may be understood, if they are clearly explained to them. In proportion as they improve, their desire of learning increases; and they frequently make sacrifices to receive instruction for a whole day. Their religion does not hinder them from embracing Christianity. They pay adoration to no being, and have no god to exchange; for they do not much regard their Torngarsuk, and do not think much good of him. It cannot, therefore, be wondered at, that they like to hear of an almighty, wise, and beneficent Being, who does so much good to mankind; that they wish to learn more about him, and promise to obey him. It is very seldom that one who has begun to take instruction goes back; but they often make visible improvement. The children, in particular, show the greatest inclination to go to school, and love of learning and diligence when they are there. They are unacquainted with constraint, as we shall see in the sequel. This by the way on their disposition to religious instructions.

The heathens like to hear of the Supreme Being, who is called God; but it must seem to be by chance. If we satisfy their curiosity, by relating to them something concerning our country, we may generally direct their thoughts upwards; for example, by saying to them, "All this we owe to a mighty and good Being, who has created and supports every thing," &c. Most of them are not wholly ignorant; but, to make them desire more particular instruction, they generally, but not always, have need of some impulse from without. Some accept invitations from their baptized relations; some come because they are embarrassed to find a lodging; others, again, out of grief on the death or murder of a friend; and others, in fine, because they are accused of witchcraft, and pursued for that reason. For such reasons many came to me to be instructed; and they related, frankly, the motives of their desire. Temporal advantages, most certainly, do not entice them to us. When baptized, they enjoy no advantages above the heathens on that account, but are even sometimes slighted, under the pretence that they are dishonest in their payments, and not to be trusted. The true reason of this is, because they are thought to be rather more prudent, and not so willing to fill the bottomless blubber tubs. But this by the bye. I will here give a short account of the nature and manner of the instruction, as well in respect to the grown-up heathens or Catechumens, whom their age and their occupations did not allow to learn to read, as to the baptized and their children.

As soon as we had, in some measure, given the former an idea of God, of his properties, and his relation to the world, we proceeded to instruct them out of the books: these were, in my time, Luther's Catechism, the first printed book in Greenland, by H. Egede, and Pontoppidan's Explanation: every sentence was read and explained to them [42]. Now the teacher read to them; the Catechumens listened attentively, and repeated, softly, what they heard (because, as has been already said, they could not read themselves); and, after some repetitions, he asked sometimes one, sometimes another, if they had understood him; whether they had retained any thing, &c. &c. These readings were continued every day; and some progress was daily made. Every thing which had been learned was gone through again, every week. In this manner, those who were docile and diligent were able, between Michaelmas and Whitsuntide, to learn by heart, and understand, the abovementioned books, with the exception of some chapters, which were explained to them afterwards. But it was not the understanding only that gained; the heart, too, was (God be thanked!) often moved. Of this we were particularly convinced on the day when the Catechumens were baptized. With proper seriousness, they gave an account of their knowledge in Christianity; with profound feeling and holy purposes, most of them pronounced their vows, and received baptism, kneeling. The baptism of the Catechumens is a true festival.

But those, who have not learned to read, must soon forget the instruction they have received, if it is not continued. For this reason, as long as the winter lasted, there were daily prayers in one of the largest Greenland houses, every morning and evening. Except on Sunday, when divine service was performed, they were called every morning to prayers, before the men went to their fishing. As soon as they were assembled, a hymn was sung, and the Catechism gone through; then a morning prayer was read, and, at the conclusion, some verses. The whole lasted about an hour. The old people were questioned from the Catechism as well as the young; and like them appeared again in the evening, at the catechization and prayers. In this manner, they not only did not forget what they had learned, but made great improvement. On Saturdays and Sundays, instead of the catechization, in the evening, one or two chapters of the New Testament were read. Thus, they had an opportunity of hearing the sacred books themselves, and they recollected the passages which proved the truths which they had learned.

When they had learned the whole explanation by heart, and expressed a wish to partake of the Lord's Supper, they were especially instructed in the intention of Jesus in founding the Sacrament; and then, if their conduct was good, admitted with their old countrymen to the Lord's table, by which they felt themselves still more bound to act with integrity. It is surprising that these people, who have grown up as heathens, are able, when baptized, to lay aside almost all their ancient superstitious opinions; and yet this is really the case. But if any should be deficient, the warning of the Minister, in private, is generally sufficient to bring them back. They promise amendment, and it is seldom, extremely seldom, that they break their word.

The Greenland children are desirous of learning, and the parents encourage them in it; they were seen to carry the little children to school, through the deep snow, and fetch them away. From nine o'clock in the morning, till two in the afternoon, I was employed in giving instruction every day except Saturday. The little ones soon learnt their letters, and endeavoured to advance farther; the bigger ones were divided into classes, according to their abilities and knowledge, and all learnt by heart, after they got home, the lesson which had been explained to them. By way of change, the latter wrote some hours every day, and, as the room was so confined, I was forced to let some read while others wrote, and the first again write while the latter read. At the age of eleven, at the most of twelve, and, sometimes, of ten, they could read any printed Greenland book readily and fluently, and could say by heart the Catechism, a part of Pontoppidan's Explanation, &c. As the latter was not printed, I wrote a copy as legibly as I could, and divided it into slips, which I laid before the children to copy, when they could write a little, and read writing with ease. Thus, several could copy the book at the same time, and which I afterwards gave them, stitched together. They looked upon it with delight, as a testimony of their improvement, and preserved it as a sacred treasure. As they often wrote letters to each other, nay even to me, they acquired more facility in writing; and, at the same time, were accustomed to think, and to express their thoughts. Thus all of them, girls as well as boys, learnt to write, while, at the same time, besides reading the books of instruction, they made themselves better acquainted with the New Testament, particularly the Evangelists, than they were in their younger years, when they read them merely to learn to read. In their thirteenth year, or when they were thirteen years old, they were discharged from the school, till they were afterwards to be instructed for the purpose of being confirmed. In doing this, there was nothing to fear; the daily examination at the hour of prayer was our security, that they would never forget what they had learned.

All this was done without the least constraint; but, as far as the children were concerned, not without encouragement. In my school journal, I noted the extremely rare cases of neglect, the greater or less degree of diligence and good behaviour, and divided among them, once a fortnight, a lispound (twenty pounds) of hard bread, as a reward and encouragement. The diligent received a loaf; those who had distinguished themselves by their improvement and good conduct, two loaves; the less diligent half a loaf; the careless and idle nothing at all. If the reward was encouraging for the former, the gentle punishment was deeply felt by the latter; and it was seldom that I had occasion to express my dissatisfaction a second time.

Among these children of nature, old as well as young, I first learned that Man is more certainly led to what is good by mildness than by severity, that rigour, harshness, and authoritative language, may produce obedience; but that love gains the heart more readily to yield it. In the long period in which I have since been in office in my own country, and in the various congregations that have been intrusted to me, I have experienced the same, though (I confess) with more frequent exceptions; but may not these more frequent exceptions be, perhaps, imputed to ourselves, and to our mode of proceeding? I, for my part, am fully convinced, that, in general, Man, when well treated, wishes to follow the good road.

Chapter XVII.

Some Cures.

The baptized Greenlanders apply to the Minister as well for internal as external diseases, and we are the more bound to assist them, as we forbid them to apply to the sorcerers. But, in my time, most of us came to Greenland very ignorant of every thing relative to this subject. We found there only a few books, such as Richter's Knowledge of Man, a book on midwifery, and one or two books of prescriptions. This was all. But that we might not kill the poor people instead of helping them, we were obliged diligently to study Richter, and to pay strict attention to the symptoms of their disorders, and the remedies prescribed for them. God knows that this part of my office cost me much trouble and frequent uneasiness, which was increased at the beginning by the circumstance that I did not understand the Greenlanders, and they did not describe their sickness in such a manner that I could with confidence prescribe for them. In such an embarrassment, and when my interpreter, my old Catechist, was not present, I more than once gave them 100 drops, and more, of strong-tea (nothing but drops would do), thinking that, if they did not do any good, they would at least not kill the patient. I cannot help smiling, even now, when I recollect, that a Greenlander one day came to me for some physic for his sick wife. He made all manner of signs, and poinded to his belly. I concluded that he wanted it for himself, counted, with a grave air [43], 100 drops of tea, mixed them with water, and was going to give him the dose: "No," said he, "it is my wife;" and went away with his drops. The next day he came to me, and said, "Thank you, Priest! It did good; she had drunk it, she was better, and now she is quite well." Thanks to their good constitutions, and their confidence in the Minister! I could mention several important cures that were effected at a later period, with insignificant, perhaps in some degree wrong, remedies; but I will mention only two, which were certainly the most remarkable.

One of the sons of the Catechist, went one day with a companion to shoot birds on the sea shore. He sat in a stooping position while his companion, who was standing a little behind him, was going to fire over him, but, instead of that, lodged the whole contents of the gun in the young man's left side. He fell, and was conveyed, as it appeared, dying, to his father's tent. I was ill, and my wife was, therefore, obliged to apply the first dressing. The next day, I crawled to him, and found him in a lamentable situation. I took off the bandage, and examined the wound. There were as many holes as there had been shot in the gun. I tried first to get out the cartridge paper, as gently as possible, indeed, but it could not be done without giving the patient great pain. I extracted only a few shot in this first operation, washed the wound with wine vinegar, laid lint, and then a plaister for gun-shot wounds upon it. He could not retain his water, and this was as black as gunpowder, which showed that the bladder was injured. I gave him Essentia dulcis several times in a day, by the use of which the bladder was cured, and the urine recovered its natural colour. I cleaned the wound every day, took out always more shot, and proceeded with the same mode of treatment. But now, all the holes ran together into one, which was about as large as a crown piece. One day, when I took off the bandage, I saw in the wound some berries, which he had eaten; nay, afterwards, even the excrements came through it: the entrails, therefore, had also suffered injury. I again gave him Essentia dulcis, and all returned to its natural order. I leave it to the gentlemen of the faculty to decide whether this remedy, or merely kind nature, had healed the bladder and entrails. I was not in a hurry with the healing of the wound, but continued as I had begun. At last, I saw new flesh, the wound became smaller and smaller, and, in eight weeks, the cure was so far effected, that the patient could walk upon crutches. In four weeks more, he could walk with the help of a stick; and, in half a year, he was as active as if he had never received any injury, rowed his Kajak, hunted the seal, and was married a few years after.

A young woman lost her child, which was but a few weeks old; she had an ulcer in one breast, which grew hard, swelled, and gave her much pain. She came to me: I applied yellow salve of marshmallow, by which she was cured in a few days. I begged her not to expose herself to the severe cold, which might bring on a relapse: but as soon as she was cured, she forgot the pain, and my warning, and went out without a cloak. The consequence was, that the breast became harder and more painful than before. As she had not followed my advice, she was now afraid or unwilling to apply to me again. Relief was necessary: she and her husband consulted together, and thought, if there were a hole in the breast, the milk might be easily pressed out, plaister might be procured, and the wound might be healed. They proceeded accordingly. The knives of the Greenlanders are always sharp, but the man whetted his, and cut a hole in the breast as long and broad as the palm of the hand, from above down to the nipple. This operation, indeed, gave the wife pain, but she bore it patiently, in the hope that she should now be able to press out the milk. But they were both soon convinced of the impossibility of effecting it. The milk was all changed into corrupt matter, and the woman could not bear the breast to be touched. "Let us go to the Priest," said her husband. "But I am ashamed to go to him," replied the wife, and remained for that day in the same state. The next day, when school was over, I went out into the open space before my house, to take the fresh air [44]. As I went out, I saw both the man and his wife in the kitchen; but as it was not unusual to see Greenlanders there, I did not regard it, nodded to them, and went on. But as they still stood there when I returned, I said, "Your breast, I suppose, is now quite well." She was silent, but the husband answered, "No! it is much worse than before." "Come in," said I, "that I may look at it." They went in. She held one hand under her cloak, to keep it from touching the sore breast; her husband helped her to take off the cloak. I was accustomed to see bad wounds, large and offensive sores, to lay plaisters on the former, and to press the matter out of the latter; but the appearance of this breast was new to me, and I doubted whether I could afford any assistance. The milk veins were cut through, and full of a tough green and yellow pus. The flesh, and the edges of the wound, were blackish. What should I do? I desired my wife to warm some spirit of camphor, with which I washed the wound, and continued to do so till all the corrupt milk was removed, nor did I forget to wash the black edges of the wound. For a long time, the woman sat insensible; but, at last, the flesh assumed a fresher redder colour, and she felt pain. Though she groaned with pain, I continued to wash the wound for some time, till I thought it was quite clean: I then laid lint upon it; and, after that, a plaister, as far as I remember, salve of melilot (Trifolium Melilotus), and visited her every day to look at her breast. Contrary to expectation, the wound soon began to be covered with a new skin, and in a month it was healed; but the woman never afterwards had any milk in her breasts. A year after this, she bore a son, whom my wife suckled, because the mother herself could not, and there was no other woman in the neighbourhood who had a child at the breast. The care which my wife bestowed on this child, was, in some measure, a reward for his father's attachment to me, for he was the same young man, who, as I have related before, came when I was struggling with the Greenlander who had attempted to stab me, and had the courage to ask whether he should help me.

After my return from Greenland, I related these cures to my friend, the late Counsellor of State, Guldbrand: he smiled, and, in respect to the remedies applied, called them miraculous cures.

Chapter XVIII.

The Avenger of his Father, or the Triumph of Religion.

The murder of a father must be revenged, however long a period may elapse before vengeance can be exercised. A son, about thirteen or fourteen years of age, was present when his father was murdered, which happened about twenty years before my arrival in Greenland. He grew up to manhood, was a very active fisherman, married, and was respected by his countrymen; but he was yet too weak to take revenge on the murderer of his father. The latter was surrounded by a numerous family; had three wives; and was, in many respects, so superior to his countrymen, that the Danes called him King. However, to obtain his end, the injured son, some years after my arrival, removed, with his family, far to the south, where most of his relations lived; because he hoped to prevail upon them to accompany him back, and, by their means, to become formidable to his adversary, and, with their assistance, to execute his design. He came to them; expressed his grief; painted the murder of his father, of which he had been a witness, and the dreadful circumstances which attended it, in the most lively colours; and persuaded them to accompany him to the north. But they were obliged to provide themselves with the necessary provisions, which, as well as the variable weather in the autumn, delayed their voyage. When he, at last, landed among us, with his relations, among whom there were some active young men, our Greenlanders had long taken up their winter abodes, and there was no room vacant. I do not remember whether his own house was so decayed that it could not be repaired in a short time, or whether others had taken possession of it. I had never seen him before, for his home was on the other side of the Isefjord; however, he came to me, and requested me to let him have a small house, which belonged to me, a quarter of a mile to the north of my baptized Greenlanders. Though I, as well as the whole neighbourhood, had heard of the cause of his journey to the south, and now saw his numerous train, I granted his request, without saying any thing to him upon the subject. In a few days the house was in an habitable condition, and large enough for them all. He soon after came, and thanked me for my kindness.

He came often, and once excused himself by saying, "You are so amiable, that I cannot keep away from you." In some of our conversations, I profited by his inclination to me; but without alluding to what he had upon his heart. Two or three weeks had hardly elapsed, when, upon one of his visits, he said that he should like to learn something about the great Lord of Heaven, who, as I told him, had created all things. "Some of my relations also," said he, "wish to learn." I had no hesitation in granting his wish and, therefore, went the following day to his dwelling, where I learned that, for the present, ten or twelve persons wished to take instruction. The others said they would wait till they heard whether it was not too difficult to learn. I had in the colony a young man of mixed race, who had considerable information, and wrote well. I engaged him as national catechist; paid him the first year myself; and introduced him into this family as their teacher. "He shall instruct you every day," said I; "and I will come to you myself as often as I can, to assure myself of your progress and your attention." "We will be attentive," answered they; "but you must come often, and we will come to you." I visited them every week, and had reason to be pleased with their attention and progress. The timidity of the Catechist vanished by degrees. He asked my advice in every difficulty, and gave me a faithful account of their domestic economy, &c. Once, when the hour of instruction was concluded, I asked two old people whether they had also a mind to learn. The woman answered, "He may, but I am blind and incapable." "For that very reason you can learn better than I," said the man:

"you may be all ear, but I am disturbed by the many people who come in and out." However, these two old people, and, at last, the whole family, came to be instructed. Kunnuk (this is the name of the Greenlander of whom we chiefly mean to speak) distinguished himself by his continual application, and extraordinary improvement. He often neglected his fishery to hear the instructions; but it was also his firm resolution to be baptized.

Spring approached, and the month of May was come; when the following conversation took place between my Greenlander and me.

He. Will you baptize me? You know that I am obedient. I know God; and my wife, as well as I, wishes to become a believer.

I. Yes, you know God; you know that he is

good, that he loves you, and desires to make you happy; but he desires, also, that you shall obey him.

He. I love him; I will obey him.

I. If you want to obey him, you must kill nobody. You know that you have often heard his commandment; "Thou shalt do no murder."

He seems confounded, and is silent.

I. Hear me, good Kunnuk! I know that you have come here with your relations to take revenge on the murderer of your father, but you must not take revenge on him, if you want to become a believer.

He (moved). But he murdered my father! I saw it, and could not help him; I must now punish him for his crime.

I. You grieve me.

He. By what?

I. That you will murder.

He. Only him who deserves to die.

I. But the great Lord of Heaven says, Thou shalt not.

He. I will not, only him.

I. But you must not kill even him. Have you forgotten how often you have heard, this winter, his command Do not revenge thyself?

He. Shall, then, the wicked murder with impunity?

I. No, that he shall not; God will punish him.

He. When?

I. Perhaps in this world; but certainly at the day of judgment, when he will reward every one according to his deeds.

He. That is such a long delay; my countrymen and relations will blame me, if I do not avenge my father.

I. If you did not know the will of God, I must let you do what your heart suggested: I must say nothing to your returning evil for evil; but now I must not be silent.

He. That is difficult! What shall I do then?

I. You shall not kill him; you shall even pardon him.

He. Pardon him! Your doctrine is very difficult.

I. It is not our doctrine; it is Christ's doctrine.

He sighs, and is silent.

I. Perhaps, too, your father was not innocent; perhaps he had also killed somebody, and deserved to die.

He. That I do not know; but then this man also deserves to die.

I. Yes, kill him; but continue to be an unbeliever; but expect that, some day, one of his children will kill you or your family.

He. Priest, you are no longer amiable! you speak hard words!

I. Kunnuk, I love you, and therefore wish that you may not sin against God, who has had you instructed in his will, and who will do justice even to your adversary.

He. Stop, then; I must talk about it with my relations.

He went; came home sorrowfully; spoke little; and ate nothing during the whole day. They observed his unusual ill temper, and asked him the cause, which he, at last, told them. I pass over the answer of his relations, and their consultation, on this subject, for many days together. The following evening I went to them, and found them all at home. Without entering into any thing relative to the conversation we had had, I chose pieces for the catechization, and from the Bible, as well as hymns, which disposed the heart to mild feelings, and invited it to placability. "Thank you, Priest" said Kunnuk, as I departed: "it was good that you came." Some days after, he again came to me: his manner, his countenance, every thing indicated a violent struggle, as well with his heart, as with his friends. I first addressed him, saying, "You are not in spirits; tell me, what have you on your heart?" "I will, and I will not; I hear, and I do not hear," answered he: "I never felt so before." "What will you?" said I; "and what will you not?" "I will forgive him," answered he; "and I will not forgive him: I have no ears, when they want that I shall revenge myself; and yet I have ears." "When you will not forgive him," said I; "when you listen with approbation to those who dissuade you from it; then your unconverted heart speaks, which demands revenge; but when you will forgive, when you will not hear your advisers, then the better part in you speaks; then God speaks to your heart. What will you now do?"

"I was so moved," answered he, "when you spoke yesterday evening; then my heart wished to obey." "See," said I; "ought you not to feel that it is the voice of your heavenly Father which spoke to your heart?" I now repeated to him the latter part of the life of Jesus; his forgiveness, his prayer for his murderers. "That was laudable," said he; and a tear sparkled in his eye: "but he was better than we are." "Yes," answered I, "infinitely better; but he will have us resemble him in this; and, if we have only a good will, God will give us strength; and we shall be satisfied with ourselves. But now you shall hear, that a man like you and me could pray for those who sought to kill him, because he declared to them the will of God, and desired them to believe in Jesus." I read to him the death of Stephen, Acts, chap. vii. He dried his eyes, and said, "The wicked men! He is happy, he certainly is with God in heaven." "Yes," continued I, "that he is; and you and every body, who acts as he did, shall also come there." "Good Priest!" interrupted he; "my heart is so moved. I will but, give me still a little time: when I have brought the other heart to silence, and am quite changed, I will come again." "Go," said I, "and pray to the good God, that he may strengthen you in your resolution; I also will pray for you." He went, and my hope was almost certainty.

At last, he came with a joyful countenance, like

him who carries peace in his heart. "Now I am happy," said he, "I hate no more, I have forgiven." "Do you, really, feel yourself happy by it?" said I. "Yes," answered he, "my heart is so easy." "You rejoice me sincerely," continued I; "but may I depend upon you? Your heart will again excite you to revenge, and your friends will tempt you." "I do not know whether this will happen," was his answer; "but I have conquered, and you may trust me." "It would be melancholy," said I, "if, after you had become a believer, you should commit this murder." "You are so suspicious, Priest!" he interrupted. "You would now commit a greater sin," continued I, "than if you had never known God, and never vowed obedience to him." "I was rejoiced," interrupted he, "but your words afflict me." "I will not afflict you," said I; "I only want to try you, whether you are able to keep what you promise. Do not trust your heart too much!" "My wicked heart shall be silent," answered he. I now asked him, what had wrought this change in him; "The energetic words," answered he, "which Jesus has taught me, and whom I will follow. I never thought that I could be disposed, as I now am. Did you not perceive how moved I was, as you read to me about him on the cross; how he prayed for his murderers, Father, forgive them, they know not what they do? Then I vowed in my heart, I, unworthy as I am, that I would forgive, and now I have forgiven. Now, I hope you will consider me and my wife, who has never hated, and who, like me, longs to become a Christian, worthy of baptism?" "Yes, good Kunnuk!" answered I, "I will baptize you and your wife, in God's name; but thank God, that he gave you an opportunity of knowing him, and his will, and forget not that you are bound in baptism to believe in him, to love him, and to obey his commandments; consequently, to leave off wickedness, and continually to become better." "I know it, Priest!" said he; "God sees my heart, and he will give me strength to remain faithful to him." He left me, full of joy and of gratitude to God. I deferred the reception of him, and the others, into our Christian community, for a fortnight; I thought it necessary to defer it, particularly on his account.

The day arrived, the whole of the divine service had reference to the baptismal act. He gave an account of his belief in Christianity, with openness and truth; he answered, with feeling, the questions from the Altar-book, and silent tears bedewed his cheeks, when he knelt down to receive baptism, in which, by desire, the name of Niels was given him. The divine service ended, as usual, with a hymn and prayers. He now came, gave me his hand, and said,

"Thank you, good Priest! I am happy." Upon this, he turned to the congregation, of whom some kissed him (this was unusual). "Receive me now as a believer! We will love each other." All answered this address with "Yes;" and now they went home together, united as persons having one Lord, one faith, and one baptism. I thanked God, with heartfelt joy, for the triumph of truth over this heart, and so many others.

After some days, he sent his enemy the following message: "I am now become a believer, and you have nothing more to fear." Upon repeated invitations, the former came one day with a few attendants. He was received in the most friendly manner, treated with the greatest kindness, and returned home in peace. Only, when he received him, my Greenlander said, "I have forgotten it." He was invited to return the visit; went, contrary to the advice of his friends, without attendants, and was received as a friend. They ate and spent the time in conversation, till they parted in the evening on the best terms; but when Niels was not far from the shore, he perceived water in his Kajak. He hastened towards land, got out, and found that a hole was cut in his Kajak. He soon stopped it up, proceeded, and arrived safe home. Some time after, he told me this, with a smile, saying, "He is still afraid, and has, without doubt, had this done for that reason; but I will not harm him." He remained constantly faithful to his vow. I even received a message from him, about ten years after my departure, saying, that he was faithful to God, and his vow.

Chapter XIX.

The Heathens kill Witches.

Perhaps there may be in Greenland, as among us, wicked witches, or persons who, by unmeaning mummeries, would injure others if they could. Some affirm it. I do not know it; but this I know, that innocent persons, on the accusation of the Angekoks, are not seldom suspected and treated as witches. These Angekoks are generally the very refuse of the people, either unskilful in the chase, or lazy.

Yet, as reputed wise men, who are connected with Torgarsuk, they possess the confidence of their countrymen, and often make use of it to ruin their innocent fellow countrymen. On occasion of sicknesses, or death, or of ill success in hunting, those, who have met with the misfortune, ask them, who may be the cause of it, or who has brought this evil upon them. Woe then to the old widow without a protector, or to the old man without grown-up sons, against whom they have a secret ill will, or whose property tempts them. They are capable of long concealing their hatred, even under the appearance of friendship; but they execute their vengeance in a cruel manner, when the measure of sin, according to their ideas, is full. They generally proceed in the following manner: The person accused and condemned is called out of his house, or his tent, with a voice with announces to him that he is to die.

He turns pale, but goes out notwithstanding, and his furious accusers now ask him the following questions: Are not you an Illiseetsok? Did you not kill such a one by your words or your malice? If the person condemned even answers. No! his death is still inevitable; but in his mortal anguish, he sometimes answers, Yes: hereupon, they stab him with their knives, cut him to pieces, and every one eats a piece of his heart, that his ghost may not return, and frighten them. In this manner, the heathens, who lived a little farther to the north, examined and killed an old man, who had been with me only a few hours before. He was then cheerful, talkative, and desirous to know what we were going to do the following day (Christmas day), as he had heard something from the baptized Greenlanders that he did not understand, and had seen that they were dressed in their best clothes. "You will not understand me either," said I, "as you are not acquainted with the great Lord of heaven and earth; but we rejoice tomorrow, because he let his Son come upon the earth, and teach us how we shall exert ourselves to become good and happy." "That is wonderful," said he; "but give me something which I can show to the others when I return home, and I will tell them what I have seen and heard." I gave him some bread and tobacco; and he left me without the smallest presentiment of what awaited him. But hardly an hour had elapsed after his return, when he was called out, and murdered in the manner above described [45].

The following morning, just as I was going to begin divine service for the Greenlanders, I was informed that a Greenlander from the north desired to speak to me. My congregation was already assembled; I, therefore, desired him to wait till divine service was over. "No, Priest," said he, "I must speak to you immediately." When he came in, he continued, "My father's brother, who was yesterday with you, was murdered a short time after he returned home. I could not protect him; but I cannot continue to live among these people. If you will receive us (we are eight, mostly children), we will remove hither, and live among the believers, who do not kill innocent persons." I promised to fulfil his desire, but it was necessary to examine first if there were room for them; and for this he had to wait. "I will readily wait," said he, "if we may but come." Some families, who had more or less room to spare, were willing to receive them. I sent him word of it. The next morning, we had them all with us, and, the following year, they were all instructed and baptized. Soon after, I went to the north, and, though the heathens do not like to hear reproofs, I called them severely to account for their conduct. "You kill wicked people in your country, I suppose?" said one. "Yes!" answered I, "but we first convince ourselves that they are wicked. The great governor in our country even gives to a certain man the commission to defend them, that no innocent person may die; but you behave like furious madmen." "You kill the wicked, so do we. But that those whom we kill are wicked, we understand better than you, Priest!" This was all the answer they returned to my reproof.

Chapter XX.

Religion and Superstition of the Greenlanders.[46]

The Greenlanders believe in a "Superior Being," and the immortality of the soul. This Being, whom they call Torngarsuk, is, according to their description, rather evil than good. He cannot be eternal, as he is said to have a great grandmother, a terrible woman, who rules over the sea-animals, often summons them to her, and thus deprives the inhabitants of their support. Neither is he considered as the creator of the world, for the world, they think, arose of itself, and the first Greenlanders grew out of the ground. Some make Torngarsuk a spirit; other say he is like a beast; others, that he resembles a man. Some affirm that he is immortal; others, that a certain noise can kill him. His abode is very deep in the earth, where living is agreeable, and provisions abundant. So different are their ideas of this being: but they neither love nor fear him; nor do they adore him [47]. When they are in health, their fishery successful, and they have nothing to trouble them in other respects, Torngarsuk is quite indifferent to them. Only when they are ill or unhappy, or the sea-animals leave the coast, they have recourse, not to Torngarsuk, but to their Angekok, who is in connection with him. The Angekok then asks his advice, and brings the answer.

They believe in the immortality of the soul, and that its state, after death, is better than the present, and happier for them all; for, according to their ideas, they will be all happy then, without distinction. They, indeed, believe that there are two places of abode after death, one in heaven, the other under the earth, but both happy: they, however, consider the subterranean abode as the happiest, where only those come who have suffered much distress in this world, or have done great services to their fellow-creatures; the souls of all the others come into heaven. The soul is, indeed, of the nature of a spirit; but it has something material about it; something delicate and soft, which may be felt. It may become sick; and, in this case, the Angekok can take away the sick part, and put something healthy in its room: it may be lost, and then he can give a new one. The northern lights are the souls of the deceased, playing at ball, in heaven [48].

The Sun and Moon were Greenlanders, and brother and sister. The sister, the sun, was extremely beautiful; and her brother, who had an illicit passion for her, pursued her every where. In order to escape from him, she fled to Heaven, where he still follows her. He is, besides, a great rogue; and women cannot be too much on their guard against him. When the full moon shines upon the water, the girls dare not drink of it, for fear of becoming pregnant [49].

Air, earth, water, and fire, have each their spirits, who exercise a certain sway, each in his own sphere. Care must be taken not to make them angry. A quarter of a mile to the north of my place of abode, there was a dangerous place for Kajak-rowers, who were sometimes upset by an invisible being. In these cases, fear did the most, and violent gusts of wind, from the east, the rest.

Apparitions and ghosts are believed in here, as they are every where. For this reason, they bind the legs of the dead, while they are still pliable, up to the hams, and carry them, in winter, out of a window, or, in summer, out of the back part of the tent, that their ghosts may not return. For the same reason as we have before related, they tear out and devour the hearts of those whom they kill as sorcerers: the fear that the spirit of the person killed should haunt them, is the true cause of this cruelty. Greenlanders are often drowned in the chase of seals; and then their spirits appear after death. They are heard to come on shore, and knock the ice from their Kajaks; nay, they are seen to carry them on shore, and lay them on the places for boats.

The rocks, also, have their spirits, which are very dangerous, as they even come down into the houses by night, and steal provisions. If it is true, as they relate, that individual Greenlanders now and then, from despair, leave society for ever, and dwell among the rocks, it is no wonder if they visit the houses, especially in winter nights, to find there something to prolong their wretched existence. Even some Greenlanders do not look on these as spirits, but as unfortunate persons, who, by being insulated from mankind, have become savage and formidable.

When any one who is accused of sorcery dies a natural death, he cannot lie quietly in his grave. A woman, who was accused of being an

Illiseetsok, was buried not far from my house. Some stones which covered the grave slipped off; the dogs found the corpse, and tore off one leg. "So it seems she was an Illiseetsok," said the Greenlanders. "Why?" said I. "Because her bones cannot lie in peace," answered they. However, I caused the leg that was torn off to be put in its place again, and the grave to be repaired. "He does not believe it," said they.

I have never heard, nor do I remember to have ever read, any thing that could lead to the conjecture that they make offerings to Torngarsuk: they do not esteem him so much. However, I was informed of an offering, which nobody in my part of the country neglected to make upon occasion. On the road to Erkame, the last inhabited spot on this side of the Isefjord, there is a large stone, on which every one who goes by lays his offering, a little meat, bacon, skin, berries, &c. I often asked to whom they gave these things: nobody knew this. "People" said they, "always used to do so." This offering must, originally, have had a meaning: perhaps it was to conciliate some spirit of the mountains, or the sea; perhaps to secure the way backward and forward, and not to be led astray.

Chapter XXI.

The Domestic Life of the Greenlander.

The Greenlanders every year, about Whitsuntide, leave their then very unclean and offensive winter habitations, to live in tents, and soon after go farther to the south, partly to catch a larger species of hallibut and herring's, partly to carry on barter with the inhabitants of the south. They return at Michaelmas, to repair and dwell again in their houses, which, during their absence, have been properly purified by the air. The men do nothing but examine the wood-work, procure what is wanting, and put it in where necessary. The women, on the other hand, must provide whatever else is required; as, for example, stones, if a wall built the year before is sunk, and earth, to fill up the intervals between the stones. When this is in order, they cover the walls inside with white skins, prepared and sewed together, lay the benches; put in the windows, which consist of the entrails of whitefish, sewed together; furnish the house with lamps, kettles, chests, tubs, &c. In this manner, the house looks, at the beginning, very neat; but the walls become dirty by degrees, and the floor is made by degrees so slippery by the seals' blood continually spilt upon it, that the feet stick to it; not to speak of the stench and the carrion flies caused by the half-picked bones, and the like, which are thrown and remain under the side benches.

Two, three, or more families generally live together in one house. Each of them knows how far its portion extends; but there are no partition walls. The women occupy the right bench, and the men the side benches: sometimes, however, men are seen on the side benches; but with this difference, that they set their feet on the ground, whereas the women sit entirely upon the bench. Here they all sit almost without clothing, the women in short drawers, about a quarter of an ell long; the men in breeches that are rather longer, and in the usual form. The bench is their bed, but the married people have their sleeping-place under it [50]. When the boys have attained the age of twelve or thirteen, they may no longer lie upon the bench among the women, but have a place to sleep on, under the windows, where they always remain till they are married. Notwithstanding their sleeping so mixed together, and their scanty clothing, no illicit passion is entertained in their houses. The married and unmarried, of both sexes, have a certain reserve towards each other, and a repugnance to every thing that violates decency. Every individual lives according to his own pleasure, and independent; but they all live in friendship and harmony with each other. In the morning, the men go out to the chase in summer in their Kajak, in winter in the sledge. Before they go out, they drink a draught of water, fill their snuff-box, and put a quid of tobacco in their mouth. Provided with this, they remain out the whole day without food, often in the severest weather, often in danger of their lives. He who has caught a seal, or in the season a whiteflsh, is received with joy by his wife. She drag's his prize on shore, and to the house, in which many help her, begins immediately to skin it, and cut it to pieces, and puts them, without washing off the blood, into the kettle, which already hangs over the lamp. The man, who, meanwhile, has put his boat, gun, &c. in their right places, now comes in, takes off his cloak, sits down, and waits patiently till the meat is ready.

These people want, besides, but little room; they are little, without clothing, and require no bed, at the most a seal's skin under them. In my time, it was generally known that the married people slept under the bench. Both the Greenlanders and the sailors who had Greenland wives spoke of it in this manner; and I myself sometimes observed it, on my journies, when I was frequently obliged to sleep in the houses of the heathens. The husband, without speaking, made a sign with his eyes to his wife, and retired to his place; she took no notice, but remained some time after he was gone, and then followed him.

Meantime he relates the adventures of the day on the chase. If there are any dried herrings in the house, some are laid before him on the ground, till the dinner is ready, and with that, and a draught of water, he satisfies the first calls of hunger. On the other hand, if he has been unfortunate in the chase, and there are no dried provisions in the house, which is often the case towards the end of the winter, he gets nothing at all, but he lays himself quietly down to sleep, in hope of better success the following day.

While the men are at the fishing places, and often suffer so much hardship, the women are very comfortable in their warm houses, if they have any thing to eat. They chat, cut out, and sew. They steep skins in the urine-tub, and, when the hair is loose, they scrape it off. I could scarcely endure the stench that accompanied this work, when I was by chance present, they themselves do not mind it. By degrees, when they are thus tanned, they continue their preparation. If they are to be white, they bleach them in the sun; if they are to be yellow or red, they dye them. The two last sorts are used for boots, and the first for cloaks. Skins which are to keep the hair on, to be used for winter dresses, do not require so much trouble. The women scrape off all the fat, or whatever else may adhere to the fleshy side: after this, they dry them, and lastly make them pliable by rubbing, before they cut them out. But the fat which is scraped off must not be lost. They make a cake of it, which looks like an omelet, and must be almost putrid before it is eaten; it must, therefore, taste as abominably as it smells.

The women are nothing less than cleanly in their domestic employments. The meat that is to be eaten is cut into pieces on the floor, and, without cleaning it the least from the blood and other impurities, put into the kettle, which they wash as little as their dishes before they use it. The dogs, sometimes, lick the kettles and dishes, that is all. I have seen a mother let a child make water in a dish, pour it out, and then, without farther ceremony, take the meat out of the kettle, put it in the dish, and present it to the guests, who eat it with a good appetite. Haddocks, and other fish, are dressed and eaten with the entrails. On one of my journeys, I had had no warm food for several days: when I received one evening two small haddocks, I asked my hostess to boil them for me for the following morning, which she very readily did;

but as she set them before me with the entrails in, I lost all inclination to touch them, and excused myself as well as I could.

They boil meat and fish an equal time, so that when the former is hardly more than half done, the latter fall to pieces. They do not know how to roast any thing. It is not true that they drink train oil. Only in case they have swallowed down a water-beetle with the water, and cannot get soon enough to the Priest for relief, they take some train oil, as an emetic, which produces the effect desired, and rids them of the beetle. This is proof sufficient that they do not generally drink it. But they steep angelica stalks in train oil. A woman chews blubber, spits it out, and continues till there is enough. In this the angelica stalks are steeped for some time, then taken out, and eaten with great appetite, by way of desert. I must here observe that this, like all the oil which the Greenlanders use in their lamps, is unboiled, white, and partly clear. It smells pretty much like raw pork, and has nothing of the disgusting smell of boiled train oil, which they cannot bear even in their lamps.

The mothers lick their children instead of washing them, and, when they comb their heads, eat without hesitation what they catch. "They bite," say they; "they must be bitten in return." It is also usual for them to revenge themselves in the following manner on their tormentors: Grown-up persons wrap the beard of a quill round a thin stick, and, while they are conversing with others, pass it down their back in quest of prey, pull it up now and then, as fishermen do their lines, and eat on the spot what they have taken. I have often been obliged to witness this, even in my own house. But, to the honour of our baptized Greenlanders, be it spoken, with many other bad habits, they lay aside this also; at least, they take great care not to do any thing in our presence which might offend us.

When the girls are fourteen years old, and above, they begin to set a value on themselves. From time to time, they wash their hair, and the Whole body, in urine. Thus they indeed become clean but, as their cloaks are washed in the same, they smell to us very disagreeably though to the Greenlanders this smell is pleasant. Young married women, who are rich in their way, and bear children, particularly boys, also wash themselves, chiefly when they pay visits, or travel. Elderly women, on the contrary, are not so particular, and become gradually more and more indifferent to dress. A widow must express her affliction, not only by her bowed head and unornamented hair, but also by the neglect of her person and dress. If, after some time has elapsed, she begins to look more clean and neat, this is a proof that she is not indisposed to marry again. But she cannot entertain any hopes of it, unless she be young, well behaved, and has borne children of both sexes, or, at least, sons.

An elderly widow in the colony, who was neither well behaved, nor a mother, fell in love with a young fellow, who was the best looking Greenlander in the place. She spoke to him in a friendly manner, without his regarding it. As he did not understand her, she so far disregarded the reserve usual in her sex in Greenland, especially to their own countrymen, that she courted him. Of course, he gave her a positive refusal; but still she did not give up her hopes. She came very modestly to me, and told me in confidence that Joergen was a bad man, who was good for nothing. "I do not believe that," answered I. "How so?" "I am ashamed to say it," continued she, "he wants to have me." "And you!" asked I. "I am afraid of him," replied she. "And for what reason?" She answered, in a very low voice, "A few days ago he attempted to seduce me." "You!" said I: "that is hard to believe. However, I will send and speak to him."

I sent for him. He was one of the young men of the colony whom I the most valued; of a good understanding, well behaved, and active. He came, and I said, "What is this I hear of you, Joergen? You want to seduce Zippora." "I!" replied he. "No, Priest, do not believe her. She is wicked, and would seduce me; but I cannot bear her. What shall I do?" "You must go away on a journey for a time," replied I;

"perhaps she will forget you. I will also speak to her." "Yes," said he, "I will take a journey. What an impudent woman!" He accordingly went away for some weeks, in which time his absence, and, above all, the ridicule of the other women, cured her. From that time she became again, what she could not be in the days of courtship, the afflicted widow, who entirely neglected her dress.

The Greenland women conceal their pregnancy as long as possible, and their delivery is generally easy: yet difficulties sometimes occur which require the presence of the Minister. Their midwives understand about as much as our village midwives did, before they were regularly instructed. If the delivery was protracted longer than usual, the husband hurried to me, saying, "Priest! come with me. My wife should be delivered; but there is no way."

I went with him, made the midwife give me the necessary information, and gave the patient every half hour Essentia dulcis, which sometimes promoted the delivery: in extreme distress, I gave thirty drops of oil of juniper in water, upon which strong and continued pains succeeded, and then the delivery, without any bad consequences for the mother or child. In this country, I dare not apply this remedy, in such cases; but happily it is not wanted. In the severest pains, no loud complaints are heard, only now, and then a sigh: but every sigh goes to the man's heart. In silence, and with his head bowed down, he sits, and accuses himself as the author of his wife's sufferings.

Chapter XXII.

The Education of the Greenlanders.

As children, especially sons, are their greatest treasure, they treat them with much care. In their earliest infancy they are naked, and carried upon their mother's back in a large cloak, which they call Amaut. When they take notice, she caresses them, and accustoms their arms to the motion which the Greenlander makes when he rows his Kajak. As they have no milk food, the children are suckled long; three or four years perhaps, but they sometimes bite their mother's breast severely: she, indeed, expresses some pain, and pinches the child in the lip, saying, "You little rogue!" but caresses it at the same time. This pinching with the nails, once caused a child to have a cancer in the lip. In vain, I attempted to check it. The cancer increased, and ate away all the flesh from the face. The child was, at length, unable to swallow down the milk, and died of hunger.

When the boys are a little grown up, the father gives them a whip, makes them a little sledge, and trains young dogs to draw it. Thus they learn by times to drive, and properly to manage the whip, a manoeuvre which an European seldom learns perfectly. In a few years, the father begins, at his leisure hours, to make a Kajak, and an oar; and if the preparations are all made, and the age of the boy allows it, the father takes him along with him in fine weather, keeps him at his side, teaches him to row, and, after he has had some practice in this, to throw the dart. When he is in some measure able to row the broad Kajak, the father makes it narrower, and thus more liable to upset, but at the same time lighter, and more manageable. He is now practised to keep himself in equilibrium with his oar; for the oar alone, and the right use of it, preserves the life of the Kajak rower: if the oar is broken or lost, he generally perishes. The father sometimes purposely lets him upset in this lighter Kajak, to make him bold, and to teach him to employ the oar, which is the means of his safety. Thus the son learns, at his father's side, to follow his profession, and in time to gain subsistence for himself and his family. In the evening, on their return home, the father praises his son; the latter hears the account, pleased indeed, but ashamed; seldom speaks of his deeds without being called upon, and rather modestly undervalues them. The mother, however, smiles with pleasure on her son.

As they never punish their children, and very seldom even reprove them, the consequence is, that they grow up in the habit of doing what they please, and sometimes refuse to obey their parents, who, however, are not angry with them on that account. Such an education does not seem to promise much good. We have therefore the more reason to be surprised at the different behaviour which they shew to their parents when they grow up. Then they respect, and love, and obey them; procure them subsistence when they are old, and are happy to contribute to their welfare. An aged father never suffers want, as long as his son has any thing;

and when the son marries, his mother, according to the prevailing custom, superintends the household concerns, as long as she can, and will, and the son's wife obeys and serves her. This change of behaviour is not a consequence of religion, for the heathens show the same. If they are asked how these capricious children become so good, they generally answer, "The people (the inhabitants of the country) are always so." Who is not reminded by this of the words of St. Paul? *(Romans ii, v. 14 and 15.)*

Of the education of the girls, there is not much to be said. They are accustomed to little domestic employments, according to their age; but their life, when young, is more uniform, conformable to their destination; they seem to feel their dependence, and willingly to submit to it. At a certain age, however, as has been observed, they begin to value themselves, to wash and adorn their hair and whole body. They are not indifferent to the other sex, but never licentious; unless it may be if a Dane pays his court to them, and promises them marriage. Notwithstanding the difference in their countenances, and their whole person, there is a mildness in their manner which soon pleases the sailors in particular: if they can once accustom themselves to the smell, the rest follows of course. I knew a servant of the Company, who was in every respect a man of good family and education; and who, after he had been some years in Greenland, felt an attachment to his servant maid, who however was not one of the beauties of the country. He liked the girl, but not the smell. But, as she came to him every day, he at last yielded to his passion. He found a remedy for the odour which was so disagreeable to him, and made use of it. He sprinkled her with scented water, first occasionally as she passed him, then more publicly, which produced the effect desired. He then asked her hand, and, as may be supposed, did not meet with a refusal. Their marriage was tolerably happy, and they had many children; but the wife always smelt afterwards of lavender water.

Chapter XXIII.

Miscellaneous Information.

Under my windows towards the south, I made a little garden, and had it surrounded with a palisade. The ground was rocky, and the earth not deep enough for the spade, nor rich enough for vegetation. In the neighbourhood I found good earth, and, with the help of my wife, brought in a basket to our garden so much as we thought sufficient. We let it lie till the next year, when I dug it up and sowed it. It was not till July that the ground was so far thawed, that it could be dug up: on the 7th, we sowed it; [51] on the 15th, the plants began to shoot up in most of the beds. So far to the north, and so near the Isefjord, a garden was an uncommon sight; but the uncommonly rapid growth which daily promised to crown our hopes, was also a singular but very agreeable sight to us. Cabbage grew extremely well. After that time, we had always a sufficient stock for the winter; but it was necessary to sow it very thin, and to pull up the plants which stood too thick; as the short summer did not admit of transplanting them. Turnips grew as large as a moderate tea-cup, lost their bitter taste, and became agreeably sweet: these, too, always throve well. Carrots in general grew not thicker than a tobacco-pipe, but preserved their usual taste. We had plenty of chervil and cresses: parsley, celery, and beans, would not grow. I sowed peas;

they shot up vigorously, and sometimes blossomed; but they did not produce any thing. I planted potatoes, but they grew no bigger than a pea. A little barley shot up quick, but the early frost destroyed it. Every autumn I gave my garden a layer of hearth ashes, which was very serviceable to it. In this manner we had, in some years, both advantage and pleasure of our little plantation; but the overflowing of the stream, as I have related in a former chapter, destroyed the garden, and carried off all the soil. However, we did not lose our courage on this account, but began our work anew, and accomplished it with greater trouble than the first time towards the end of summer, so that we were able to sow the garden the following year. But that was the only year that we enjoyed the fruits of it. We left Greenland, and almost a year elapsed before my successor arrived. How he found the garden, which had been so long without an owner, and what became of it afterwards, is unknown to me.

II.

Both land and sea are covered, during the greatest part of the summer, with a disagreeable fog, and in winter, before the ice is hard, with frozen vapours; but notwithstanding this, the climate is healthy, and but few diseases are known there. The Greenlanders, indeed, sometimes suffer by hemorrhage, which is painful, but not so contagious, nor so fatal, as among us. They have, sometimes, spitting of blood. The latter shortens the life; with the first they may suffer many years: during my time, one died of diabetes. Their external diseases are particularly swellings, which are dispersed by plaister of melilot, very bad boils, which, if they are not sufficiently pressed out, and carefully healed, spread from one place to another; and weak eyes, particularly in old age. However, they do not grow old even when they die on the sick bed, and many are drowned. A man of fifty years of age generally looks as infirm as if he were near seventy. As the women often grow older, and at the same age enjoy better health, if they do not entirely neglect themselves, it is probable that the many hardships which the men endure almost daily in their fishery, are the principal cause of their early old age and death. Contagious diseases, however, carry many away, grown-up persons as well as children. In a foregoing chapter, I have related the symptoms of them but I know not by what name to call them.

If I except the scurvy, the Europeans are subject to no other diseases which can be ascribed to the country or the air; and the remedies against it are, constant exercise and cochlearia. As the Greenlanders make no use of this plant, and are not tormented by this disease, one might be tempted to think, that kind Providence had caused it to grow for the Europeans, who are greatly in need of it. The scurvy is a singular disorder. It can be a long time in the body without occasioning any inconvenience, except a kind of lethargy; but if the patient does not use cochlearia, and take daily exercise, especially in the beginning, he may fall into a slumber under it, and never more awake. Sometimes it causes a not unpleasant irritation, an excitement, if I may call it so, in the very marrow of the bones, and then it is high time to apply the remedies, if the use of them has been neglected. The gums swell, and detach themselves from the teeth, which become loose, if they do not fall out. When the scurvy at length breaks out in brown and yellow spots on the legs and thighs, and makes them as hard as a board, the patient is generally saved; but he must be extremely careful to use the cochlearia, and take exercise when he has it in his power. I was not much subject to this disorder, but, as my daily occupation allowed me only one or two hours to walk about on Saturdays, and as I generally suffered in the winter from another disorder, which hindered me from taking much exercise; I was, sometimes, attacked by the scurvy, and can, therefore, describe it from experience. One fine day, we resolved to pay a visit to the Provost Sverdrup, and, accompanied by a Greenland boy, went over the Isefjord, between the icebergs. While we were on the way, an iceberg, about half a mile from us, fell, and, in a few minutes, the solid ice under us broke. "To land! To land!" cried the boy, and ran: the Clergyman ran with him: of course, I would not remain behind. But as I was hastening to get over a broad cleft, which the falling of the iceberg had caused, the scurvy held me fixed to the ice, so that I could not stir from the spot: I was, therefore, obliged to submit to my fate, and await the event. After an interval of ten or twelve minutes, I was again able to walk slowly; reached the land, at last, over clefts and pieces of ice; and gave my companions a gentle, but well merited re-proof.

III.

My salary was 150 dollars Danish currency per annum; and the allowance of provisions for myself and my wife, was, per week, ten pounds and a half of bread, three pounds of butter, two pounds of bacon, two pounds of stockfish, one eighth of a bushel of peeled barley, and the same quantity of pease. Besides, fifty dollars per annum were allowed me for coffee, sugar, brandy, wine, and groceries in general. It may be easily imagined, that, in a country where money is unknown, and the daily necessaries of life must be procured by barter, it was necessary to be very economical; but it was often impossible. I will say nothing of the assistance which the Greenlanders now and then required; but the hospitality introduced among the Europeans, consumed a great deal. In winter, the servants of the Company have no employment. They, therefore, continually drive from one place to another to pay visits, and at every place, if it is possible, are joined by new companions, and, at last, make a caravan; the true object of whose journeys is, in fact, to kill time, to enjoy good cheer in the houses of others, and to give them good cheer in return, but which has otherwise great advantages. In the colonies where there is a clergyman, a merchant and an assistant, each take part in giving the entertainment, which was thus no great burden to any of them. I, on the other hand, was alone at Claushavn, bore alone the cost of the entertainment, but also had alone the honour of showing my hospitality. Hence, and from our limited income, arose the long fasts, which I have mentioned before, and which others, it is true, also felt, but not in the same degree as we.

We were, however, never in Want of the first necessaries of life; for if the portions allowed were not sufficient, as was often the case [52], we could obtain the rest upon account. But these portions were often very moderate, sometimes not to be eaten. Among many causes, a principal one is, that the provision must be one year in the country before we dared to touch it. This precaution protected us against want, in the event of a ship's being lost; but the consequence of it was, old and often bad provisions. One year, in particular, the bread (or biscuit called skonrogiie) was so full of spiders and cobwebs, that we were obliged always to have a whisk by us when we were eating. The butter was frequently not fit to eat: in our country, it would have been regarded as common grease. The bacon and the meat were often rusty and yellow; only hunger and custom could make them go down. Happily, we took the two last articles seldom, because they promote scurvy; and though the butter was often very indifferent, yet, at other times, it was better, and we were contented. In winter, we had no want of fresh provisions. I could, in some measure, reckon upon a hare every week: we had snow-fowl (ryper) in abundance, and haddock almost every day. In summer, on the other hand, we were forced to be content with young sea mews, if we wished to taste fresh meat; but then, besides haddock, we had trout, and salmon trout, the former from the fresh water lakes, the latter from the mouths of the streams and rivers. One summer, we went ourselves to a place, some miles from the colony, to catch salmon trout, and staid there ten or twelve days. The winter before, my wife had made two fishing-nets: I and a Greenlander spread the nets, and attended to the fishery, while my wife and two maids were employed in salting and smoking. Some of the fish were indeed small, but we caught them of the weight of eight, nine, and even of ten pounds, and in such numbers, that we had enough for our friends in the neighbourhood, who could not take part in the fishery themselves, and had even some to spare for our friends in our own country.

IV.

The arrival of the vessels from our native country gave us much pleasure: we then received news from our relations and friends, the newspapers for a whole year, books, &c; our wants were supplied, and our fasting season ceased. This joy was, however, often lessened and embittered by brandy and drunkenness. The sailors having been long deprived of that liquor, were, therefore, not able to bear so much, and drank more. Nay, I even saw now and then a Greenlander drunk on these days, and, to be thoroughly intoxicated once or twice, is sufficient to destroy the health of a Greenlander for ever. Disorders sometimes ensue. Thus, two drunken sailors would once have certainly killed one of the sons of the Catechist, had not the courage of my wife saved him in time. Being in the kitchen, she heard a noise in the room of the man-servant, and asked a Greenlander who was present, what it meant: he said, they were angry with the young man, and were, certainly, going to kill him. Without informing the assistant, from Christianshaab, and me (which would have caused a delay, though we were near), she said to the Greenlander, "Help me to force open the door!" He did so; she rushed in, pushed the drunken men aside, raised the young man, who was almost strangled, and untied his neckcloth, by which he was enabled to breathe freely, and was saved. Now, but not before, she perceived she was wounded in the arm, and bleeding (a third drunken man had endeavoured to hold the door fast inside, and prevent her entering): she then bound a handkerchief round her arm, and came afterwards to us, but did not mention what had happened. It was not till some days after, when the worst of these sailors had been guilty of insubordination, and was condemned to be sent home, that she related the circumstance. Such, and similar events, naturally lessened our joy; but we did not see the departure of the ships with indifference. We remained solitary and forsaken. A whole year lay between us and our country; we looked forward to the yet hidden events of a whole year. But these involuntary feelings were but the feelings of a moment. What every year made a more lasting impression, was the departure of the Sun, about the 26th of November.

A few days before, I ascended the rocks at noon, to behold the Sun once more; and when, on the 26th, he just showed his faint but mild light, before he vanished for a long period, I sorrowfully bade him farewell. The days immediately succeeding were still tolerable; but, in December, it was twilight even at noon. At that hour, I could scarcely read a book, when standing at the window. Of course, the candles were always kept burning. The rivulet roared, the stormy sea beat against the rocks, on which my dwelling stood, and frequently dashed its spray against the windows: the dogs howled [53]. I was often indisposed. In short, every thing combined to make these weeks unpleasant: but I found that employment is a sure remedy against ennui, and, weak as I was, I had, both morning and evening, employment enough. When I travelled at Christmas to Christianshaab, we were assisted by the light of the Moon, if the sky was clear, and by the cheerful nothern lights, which often seemed to float close by us. The reader may conclude from this, with what heartfelt joy we saw the Sun return. On the 12th of January, if the weather was fine, we could see its light on the high rocks, and, on the 13th or 14th, I saw himself, glorious, and as if new created, but only for a few moments. We now felt as if we had conquered all the troubles of the year, as if we had recovered health and life. Our thoughts seemed more clear; hope looked forward to spring, summer, and ships, all happy prospects: we even seemed to breathe more freely. Here (in Denmark) we value too little the daily presence of the Sun, because we are never deprived of it. When we complain of the short days in December, let us think on the dark days in Greenland, and thank God for the December light.

According to the ordinance of the Creator, an indemnity was due to us for the long absence of the Sun, and we obtained it. After the 24th of May, he did not again set at night, rose till the summer solstice, higher and higher, and then declined a little every night; and, about the 20th of July, dipped again, at night, under the horizon. This dipping was, at first, imperceptible; only the night frosts put us in mind of it. It would scarcely be believed, that water which was boiled on the 24th of July (which was a very warm day), at five o'clock in the afternoon, could be covered with a crust of ice at eleven o'clock the same evening; and yet this was the case. I saw both the boiling of the water, and the ice upon it.

The Greenlanders and the Europeans generally travel by night, while the Sun is up; for then the sky is clear, the air generally calm, the coolness agreeable. The days, on the contrary, are foggy, the heat violent, and the bloodthirsty gnats a real torment. Towards the solstice, it seems to me that the Sun, both in its height in the sky, and its warmth, is much the same as in this country at noon in December.

It was a fine sight to behold him proceed from the west to the north, thence to the east, and again reascend from the east in majesty and splendour. The daily change of heat and cold, or at least coolness, after sunset in summer, deserved more attention, in respect to clothing, than we thought fit to pay to it. However, few seemed to suffer by their indifference.

V.

A violent storm from the south-east occasioned a Greenlander to come to me. "It is terrible weather," said he. "Yes," answered I, "it is good that all the Kajaks are come home." "This night," continued he, "I dreamt that the air and sea became so stormy; it was a strange dream." "How so?" asked I. "It appeared to me," answered he, "to blow violently from the south-east; the sea was greatly agitated; the heavens moved; and the earth quaked. Upon this, the heavens opened, and I saw our Redeemer. He was extremely glorious to behold: his eyes resembled the Sun, but I did not see any body. When he appeared in the air, I heard a loud noise; the earth was broken into pieces, and sunk into the abyss. Upon this, it appeared to me as if every body was brought before him. The multitude was very great: and I heard him say to the believers, "Fear not; I am come to redeem you!" I now awoke, full of astonishment and terror at what I had seen and heard, awaked the others in the house, and related to them my dream. Now, as there is such a terrible storm to-day, they are all much afraid, particularly my wife. "Tell me, Do you think that the world shall now be at an end?" He waited for my answer, in order, as he said, to be able to satisfy his family, by my words, and received it.

VI.

I was for a fortnight constituted Bishop, of which the following was the occasion. A young Clergyman, who supported himself and his family by giving private lessons, in a town in Fuhnen, met with Hans Egede's account of Greenland. He had scarcely read it when Egede's spirit, as it were, animated him; he wished also to serve in Greenland, and follow Egede's steps. With this intention, he wrote to the younger P. Egede, to be employed in the Mission; but received for answer, that there was no room for a Seminarist, and that it would be difficult for him, as a married man, to live at Copenhagen, while he was preparing himself, as far as possible, for the office of a Missionary. Dissatisfied with this answer, he travelled to the capital, and presented himself to the Missionary College, which he entirely gained in his favour. He said, that it was the same to him whether he went to Greenland as a Clergyman or a Catechist, if he only went there, and could be of service. He was sent to me, for the purpose of becoming a Catechist at Christianshaab, because they thought that I should do justice to his merit; and recommended him to my care and direction, adding that, from a particular and remarkable impulse, he had desired to be employed in the Greenland Mission; and that it would depend upon my testimony the following year, whether the College would propose him to his Majesty as a Missionary. As he was wholly unacquainted with the language, a year would, certainly, not be sufficient for him to learn something himself, and, at the same time, give proofs of his ability to instruct others: however, I cannot deny him docility, and attention to my advice. After the lapse of a year, I gave him a good testimony the College expected it so. I wrote, indeed, nothing more than the truth, but every thing that I could write with truth; and the consequence was, that, the year following, this College gave him the appointment from his Majesty of Missionary, and sent me the order to examine and ordain him; to place him as a regular teacher at the colony at Christianshaab, in order, as it was said, to give me some relief in my many official journies to that place, which journies were, probably, the cause of my continued indisposition. However kind this appeared to be, the real cause was, that no Missionary place was vacant, and it was determined that the man should be employed, and act independently; for, when he was removed some years after, to Egedesminde, I was obliged again to take upon me the colony at Christianshaab. I had lately been ill, and, therefore, refused to take upon me this labour, which now no longer concerned me; but they did not cease to persuade me, and I was forced to give way.

The preparation, as well as the act itself, were performed entirely according to the Ritual, and the other regulations. The inhabitants of the colony, the crews of the ships, and the Greenlanders, had never seen the consecration of a Priest. It pleased them very much, but no part of it gave them such extraordinary satisfaction as the Latin mass, of which they did not understand a word. I had translated those prayers, which, in this case, seemed to be the best; but both my colleague, whom I had requested to be present at the ordination, and he who was to be ordained, were of opinion that I was not entitled to take this liberty. Some days after the ordination, I gave him his appointment, introduced him, as Provost, the next Sunday, and sunk back to what I really was, and what I may still feel a certain satisfaction in remembering to have been [54]. After a residence of a few years, our man left Greenland, was well received, obtained, as a reward, a good living in a town in Jutland, became Provost, and died.

VII.

The Greenland children are as white when they are born as ours; but they have a blue spot in the skin, upon or above the loins, about three quarters of an inch in diameter. When they grow up, this spot extends gradually over the whole body, and is, perhaps, the cause of the rather darker colour of it. I had often an opportunity of seeing these spots, as the Greenland women, at the time of my arrival, brought their new-born children, according to the custom, naked, to be christened.

Though we daily saw naked children, yet this nakedness was very disagreeable to me in a religious ceremony. My wife, therefore, made a decent christening-dress, which was put on every child that was to be baptized. On such occasions, when she spread a handsomely embroidered altar-cloth, of nankeen, over the table, procured and made by herself, lighted
55 the candles for the communion, and daily carried, with the servant, before and after school-time, the benches in and out, or, when I was absent or ill, dressed the wounded, and, after my direction [56], gave them medicine; or, in the hardest winters, distributed bacon and meat to poor widows and children; I called her, with a certain sacred pleasure, The Servant of the Church. The good Phebe *(Romans,*

chap, xvi, verse 1 and 2) scarcely deserved this name more than she.

VIII.

The Green Islands, which lie about eight miles from Claushavn, and which I often visited on my journies of business to the south, have some resemblance with Denmark. The rocks are not high, but green, and covered with grass, like the vallies. The eye dwells with pleasure on this verdant carpet. The shore is covered with what is called silver sand, of which we always took home a good quantity. It does not shine as our silver sand does, but it contains particles of iron; and I must be much mistaken if these rocks do not contain iron. Perhaps they would deserve to be more accurately examined, especially as Norway does not belong to us now.

IX.

The island of Disco has coals, the veins of which are said to extend far into the sea. They are not of the usual kind, but are lighter, more flaky, and do not give, indeed, such a strong heat as the English, but burn clear, and have not the disagreeable smell that coals generally have. Shortly after my return, it is said to have been proposed to examine and open these mines, and, at least, to procure from them sufficient fuel for the supply of the colonies; but I do not know whether the proposal was carried into execution, or whether the produce would pay for the expense.

X.

Angelica grows on Disco island, and there only in the whole bay. The Greenlanders use, particularly, the stalks, and put them, as is mentioned above, in fresh blubber, which they chew and then spit over it; and we use, especially when we visit the sick, or on other occasions, the dried roots to chew. The former relate that a great enchanter, in ancient times, came in his Kajak, and towed the island of Disco, from the south into the bay, merely for the sake of this plant, of which the people in this country were in want. They even show a hole in a rock, in which he fastened his tow-rope. It is very singular that the Greenlanders call this plant, as the Norwegians do, Qvane; perhaps they have the name from the ancient Norwegians.

XI.

I sometimes botanized, and had several good and well preserved specimens of the plants in the neighbourhood; but as I was not versed in the science, and my collection was not complete, I left it to my friend and neighbour, Provost Sverdrup, who had a beautiful Herbarium; and he found, among the plants which I had gathered, several varieties, though they had grown so near to his own. My old friend Professor Fabricius has communicated much interesting information in this branch, as well as in many others, relative to the Natural History of Greenland, in his Fauna Gronlandica, which is known and esteemed in foreign countries.

XII.

His Royal Highness the Hereditary Prince Frederic had graciously given orders, that the Captain of a whale-ship should touch at the colony of Claushavn, and take me and my family with him, and treat us in such a manner, as he could answer for at his return. But the Directors had, at the same time, fixed his departure from Greenland, which was necessary, on account of the plan that they had then in view. It was, that the captain, after his return home, should be back in Greenland before the beginning of the winter, in order to winter there, and be able to go out so much the sooner in the spring, on the fishery. Unluckily, the ice lay this year long in the gulph; time passed away, and he was obliged to sail home without being able to reach us. I had been very weakly the preceding winter, and the return to my country, for which I really wished, was necessary for my health; I was consequently very much discouraged for some moments, when I heard that my hopes were disappointed. I now, for the first time, saw my wife very sorrowful, and unresolved, when she thought on the future; but nothing was to be done here, but to resign ourselves up to the will of Providence. In the meantime, to keep up her spirits, I said, "We will make a journey to Holsteinburg: perhaps we shall meet there with a ship, and then we can go home; if not, we shall revive our spirits among our friends, and collect strength for the approach of winter." I made my resolution known to Provost Sverdrup, who approved it, and also promised, that he and my catechist would take care of my mission till my successor arrived. He also promised, that he and his wife would accompany us some miles on our intended journey. Those of my Greenlanders who were still in the place, as soon as they heard of my resolution, declared that they would not lose me. But the day for our departure came: I still remember the moment when I got into the boat, after having taken a most cordial leave of them. They all stood there with tears in their eyes, as if forsaken: even my old, honest assistant, the Catechist. I looked at them, not without some self-reproach, but necessity commanded. I prayed for God's blessing on all present and absent, and ordered the boat to put off from shore; but I did not feel at ease.

We arrived at Egedesminde: my worthy friend could not accompany us any farther; but he absolutely would not permit me, as it was my intention, to travel without any companions [57]. His care procured us a family, who were going a part of our way to the hollibut fishery; and the company of this family, next to God, was our deliverance. Our last farewel was affecting and cordial. Both of us felt that we should miss each other [58]. My women's boat was indeed heavily laden with our most necessary things, in case an opportunity should offer to return home; but the very mild weather gave us courage to pass over a creek about a mile broad, without keeping close in shore. This was in itself no great risk, if there had been nothing else in the way; but in sailing into the creek, we had touched, though very gently, upon a shoal. The collision made a hole in the bottom of my boat, it let in water, and continually became heavier. The others, in the women's boat, which was ahead of us, called out to us, when we were in the middle of the creek, "You are sinking!" They turned round, laid their boat alongside of us, and said, "Come in, Priest, with your wife and son, or else you will be gone." "Shall we then be saved?" asked I: "shall all these people, who on my account are in the same danger, perish? I will not purchase our lives so dearly, but will quickly throw all my things overboard, and thus the boat will be lightened." "No! no!" cried they. "Come! we can take so much into our boat, that they may lade out the water: if we then immediately take it in tow, there will be no danger; because, if the boat at last sinks near the shore, we can save the people." During this conversation, a part of my goods were already taken into their boat, and we immediately got into it. The steersman unladed the water, the women rowed, the others towed, and so we reached the land within a cable's length, when my boat sunk. The people escaped unhurt; but the things which were still in the boat were so soaked by the water, that we were obliged to stop a whole day to dry every thing, even the books, upon the rocks. As soon as this was done, as well as circumstances would admit, and our boat repaired, we again put off from shore, and at last arrived at Holsteinburg, where we were received with sincere joy; and during the space of some weeks, we enjoyed here, in a circle of relations and friends, many pleasures that refreshed us, both in body and mind.

A small fishing vessel had been in the harbour, and was expected to return before its final departure: it came, and the captain was willing to take us with him. On the 23d of August, we took the tenderest leave of our friends, and went on board. The wind was favourable, the anchor was weighed, we were soon in the open sea. For the most part, the wind was pretty good, but sometimes violent. If I except, that my wife was the whole time sea sick, and that I myself one day, when the sea ran high, was nearly washed overboard, by venturing to a place where I had nothing to do, we met with no remarkable accident before we reached Hetland. For several days we had not seen the sun at noon, and therefore did not exactly know where we were. The captain, the pilot, and two or three sailors who had passed examination as pilots, pricked a chart, and it appeared afterwards that they were tolerably correct. On the 20th of September, the captain said to me, "According to our reckoning, we must see Hetland to-day." "Towards noon, we in fact got sight of land; but, in the fog," it looked like a little island in the clouds. The captain maintained that it was Hetland; the others doubted it, and took it rather to be the Orkney Islands. The majority of voices was followed, and the course changed accordingly; but the captain at the same time put a sailor in the mast, and another in the forepart of the ship, to be on the look out, and to give notice. At four o'clock in the afternoon, while the captain was sitting in the cabin, with his chart before him, the two sailors cried out, "We are close to land!" The captain was on the deck as quick as lightning, and I followed him to learn our situation. Hetland lay before us; but it was on the east side, which is a perpendicular wall of rock, and from this we were scarcely two cables length distant, and besides surrounded with numerous shoals. The captain immediately gave orders to tack, and the heavy laden ship obeyed the helm with astonishing quickness. We tacked between the shoals, and came, God be praised, again into the open sea. Ten minutes later, it would have been impossible to save us. The captain's reckoning was therefore the most correct; the opinion of the majority is not always to be depended on. On the following morning, we took the course which he was going to take the day before, namely, to the west of Hetland, and came, with variable winds, through the North Sea by Skagen [59], cast anchor off Gilleleie [60], and on the following day off Hornbek, where we let ourselves be put on shore, as the wind continued unfavourable. On the evening of the same day (the

3d of October) we came from Elsinore to Copenhagen, where I was received by most of my superiors with evident coolness.

The end.

Footnotes:

(1) Volquard Boon, a whale-fisher, of the island of Fcebr, gives the following account of a bay on the east side: "From the 21st of June till the 31st of July, 1761, he came along the coast from 76 30' to 68 40', north latitude, at the distance of from one and a half to six miles from the coast, the direction of which he found by the compass to be north-east and south-west. On the 27th of July, in the latitude of 70 40', he was carried, by a strong current, into a great bay, the breadth of which he estimated to be fifteen miles, and the direction of which was north-west by west. He could not perceive the end of the bay; for, though the air was clear, no land was to be seen (i.e. beyond it); and he therefore conjectured, especially as the stream flowed up the country, that this bay, in which there was a pretty strong current and a consid-

erable quantity of ice, probably intersected the country entirely."

Wormskjold conjectures that this bay is that which the ancients called Allum lengri Fjordz (the longest bay of all), one of the most easterly, which was narrow before, but broader farther from the mouth, along which they had built no habitations, and the end of which was unknown to them. As the stream in the Isefjord, on the west side, always flows outwards, there arises almost more than a conjecture, that this and the abovementioned bay have a connection with each other.

(2) Our learned O. Fabricius denies the green colour: see his essay on Drift Ice in the Northern Seas, in the new Collection of the Writings of the Royal Danish Society of Sciences, vol. 3, page 67; but Crana, in his History of Greenland, page 35, agrees with Roe.

(3) A remark communicated to me, by a friend, which was occasioned by the above account, makes the following explanation necessary.

(4)In this gulph, they catch, in winter, a kind of turbots, which are indeed much smaller.

(5) The fork supports the edge of the boat, in order that, while they are sewing it, or by drying in the sun, it may not get out of shape (which might easily happen, as the boat is quite wet from the voyage): three or four such props support the boat, and they are as indispensible on a voyage in a women's boat, as fat, needles, and thread, and a kind of pitch, to strengthen the seams. It was with one of these props that the boy gave the blow upon the boat which produced such unhappy consequences.

(6) Cranberries grow here in abundance, and, as far as I know, nowhere else in Disco Bay.

(7) The same anecdote is related of Thorgils Orrabeinstjupa, but with other circumstances. Cranz speaks (p. 331 and 322) of this Thorgils in the following words: "Fresh colonies continued to arrive from Iceland and Norway, who were, in part, Christians: among them was Thorgils, a new but zealous Christian, who had gone to Greenland against the repeated warnings of his former idol, and of whom they relate a strange and wonderful history of many years' persecutions by the Devil, and severe misfortunes by water and by land; after which, he at last, like Job and Tobias, obtained honours and happiness." Setting aside that part which conforms with the inclination of the ancient inhabitants of the north, like other nations, to believe in prognostics, and to regard

dreams, the contents of the Floamanna Saga are not so strange and marvellous, but very credible. In the writings of the Scandinavian Literary Society, vol. 7, there is a translation of this very interesting Saga, by Professor B. Thorlacius.

(8) A nickname, given to signify the small stature and weakness of the Greenlanders, in comparison to the tall and robust Norwegians and Icelanders. Skroelling still means, in the Danish, weak, puny.

(9) It is, however, probable, that the black death was the first and principal cause of the neglecting of the intercourse with Greenland, and of the extirpation of the Icelandic and Norwegian settlers. This plague, which raged about the year 1350, carried off about two-thirds of the population of the north. One consequence was, that navigation in general, and consequently that to Greenland also, was very much diminished in the succeeding period. The greater part of the inhabitants of Greenland were, doubtless, carried off by this plague; consequently, the articles for trade must have been much diminished, and the trade itself wholly declined. Political troubles contributed to check the little intercourse that was still kept up. Meantime the savages who came to Greenland, long after the Normans, advanced farther; and it could not be difficult for them to overpower the diminished population, now

left entirely to its own resources.

(10) According to Lieutenant Egede's Chart, the least distance from Iceland is sixty-seven miles.

(11) The late H. Egede, after his return from Greenland, not only made similar proposals for the re-discovery of the east coast, of which he speaks in his Natural History; but be even offered to go with the expedition, if it should be land, and the possession of it, even without inhabitants, would be a real addition and advantage to our country: with inhabitants, perhaps more would be gained. Religion would accompany us thither, and spread her beneficent light, with purer splendor than it formerly shone there. May this happen!

(12) So the Greenlanders pronounce the Danish word Proett (Priut).

(13) Exclamation of surprise.

(14) This happened, when, after having with infinite pains gained the top of the rock, I seated myself on the sledge to descend, which, acquiring velocity from the steepness of the descent, was hurried past the dogs.

(15) The Greenlanders, accustomed from their youth to climb up high rocks, have a great advantage.

(16) He was a good honest Jutlander, and had kept a shop in some town in Jutland. Having been unfortunate in business, he was obliged to go to Greenland, and served me, for several years, with fidelity, and uncommon zeal.

(17) That is, the time when the stock of provision was exhausted, and the arrival of the ships anxiously expected. It often lasted long, and was hard enough to bear.

(18) The overflowed stream rushed furiously between my house and the Greenlanders. The ice was the only way by which we could reach them.

(19) A pole about six feet long, with an iron at the end, which is carried to examine the ice with.

(20) When the Greenlander had helped me out, he called the dogs to him, and they swam over with the sledge.

(21) This, however, is after the reports of others. I can not affirm

it as certain, and it must be indifferent to the reader who carried it on. The Greenlanders, on the other hand, had to pay, for an ell of kersey, a pound of powder, six harpoon irons, two scraping knives, &c, a tub of blubber. The tub called a bulge was the measure in which the merchant received the blubber, and it should contain a barrel.

(22) Unicorn (Eenhjorning, Narhval) is a fish which is from sixteen to twenty-two feet in length, and has a long tooth projecting from the left side of the upper jaw. This tooth is what is called unicorn's horn.

(23) The prices in marcs and schillings are probably in paper currency, and the groschen silver currency.

(24) The rifle gun was the most important necessary. They had to pay, in the same proportion, for other necessaries; but I cannot exactly say what they gave for a kettle, for instance.

(25) The Greenlanders receive, as I have said, according to the company's tariff, only one rixdollar for a barrel of blubber, and, after the merchants' tariff, one rixdollar for one tub or barrel; but I do not know what payment was given them for whalebone, skins, unicorns horns, and other goods.

(26) The blubber sent home was calculated according to casks, each containing two barrels; the quantity, reckoning that from Jakobsbavn, was, perhaps, three hundred barrels, and above.

(27) At the place where I lived, I could not make any legal advantages, and I never allowed myself to make illegal ones.

(28) This girl did not scruple to acknowledge her attachment to her lover. She was the first, and the only one, who did so, in my time.

(29) That is, those parents that are baptized: among the heathens it is different, as has been remarked before.

(30) I must here observe, that some Greenlanders told me the young people had began too familiar an intercourse; and, at the same time, begged me to prevent, in time, further offence being caused, &c. This was a duty the more incumbent on me, as teacher of religion and morals, as the Greenlanders themselves, even the heathens, consider temperance in all things, essential.

(31) Not having room in ray house, I kept my turf in the open air.

(32) At this time, I always chewed a piece of Angelica root, as an antidote.

(33) There is a smaller kind of whale with teeth.

(34) As a husband, the deceased was the more worthy of praise, because he continued to love his wife, though she was barren.

(35) The flesh of the white fish looks like beef; it yields a barrel of blubber, or more, according to its size.

(36) The only national musical instrument of the Greenlanders is the drum, which consists of a wooden hoop, a finger board, and has a thin skin drawn over only one side of it. It is about an ell in diameter, and has a handle. The Greenlander strikes it with a stick, on the lower edge. It formerly played a conspicuous part in the mummeries of the Angekoks.

(37) An honour, which, in my time, was not shown to any servant of the company.

(38) At first, most of the sailors do not find the girls of the country to their taste; but the daily sight, want of Danish girls, and

leisure, soon make them appear tolerable.

(39) This wind brings such a degree of warmth with it, that the snow melts in the middle of winter: the lower rocks appear black, and the vallies green; but it is so violent and tempestuous, that people who are in the open air must throw themselves upon the ground, that they may not be carried away, or thrown down, when the gusts come. The thick strand ice breaks into larger and smaller pieces; and soon the open sea appears, where, a short time before, there was firm footing on the ice for many miles. All this is the work of a day; nay, sometimes of only a few hours.

(40) Here, a well meant expression.

(41) In the beginning, the Ministers were obliged to distribute, in such cases, every thing necessary, for the account of the Missionary College; but this liberality had long ceased. To receive provisions twice a week is, certainly, not enough for support; but we here see, that not only life, but also a certain degree of strength to work, was preserved. Perhaps the Danish provisions are more nourishing for these people than their own.

(42) I left this business, in the first years, to my old Catechist, who was not alone a well informed man, but also spoke the lan-

guage like a native.

(43) Not like a quack, to give myself importance, but not to excite suspicion by smiling while I counted the drops.

(44) I might well stand in need of fresh air, after having given lessons for five hours, in a small room, just high enough to allow of my standing upright under the beams, and crowded with forty or fifty children, in greasy cloaks.

(45) A son, as we have said above, owes vengeance to his murdered father. This is a private or family matter; but the murder of witches or sorcerers is an act of justice, due to the public good.

(46) This chapter, like the others, is taken from my notes on Greenland. Hans Egede, my mother's father, has said almost the same. This agreement must be a security for the truth of the statements it contains.

(47) But they obey him when they receive orders from him through their Angekoks.

(48) The Greenland way of playing at ball is a serious combat. Towards the spring, the inhabitants of two large districts form two

bodies; each tries to catch the great ball, which is thrown out, and to hinder the adverse party from obtaining it, which seldom passes without wounds, that are often mortal: those who get possession of the ball drive off in their sledges, at full speed. If they secure the ball, they are victors, and have a right to insult the vanquished, who must bear all their sarcasms with patience. Formerly, they were obliged to give up their most valuable property.

(49) Water is the beverage of the Greenlanders: they lay themselves down, and quench their thirst where they find it.

(50) The bench is not much more than half an ell from the ground; but, in building the house, the Greenlander makes the floor under the bench lower than the other part.

(51) But not every year so late. Another year I could sow on the 30th of June; one year, even the 7th: but then the plant did not come up before the 26th.

(52) Some part was obliged to serve, instead of money, to purchase fish, game, &c.

(53) The Greenland dogs do not bark loud, but only growl sometimes; but tbey howl every day at certain hours. They then as-

semble in troops, and turn their snouts up in the air. At first, this howling is abominable and deafening; but, afterwards, one gets used to it, and even finds it amusing. It lasts about a quarter of an hour; after which the Company breaks up.

(54) Soon after our return from Greenland, we were invited to a family party, in which there was one of my early friends. The company wished to know something about Greenland, and our adventures there; and we related. In the middle of the conversation, my friend whispered in my ear (but loud enough to be heard), with much self-complacency: "But, did you do any good in Greenland." I cannot describe my feelings at this question, only I remember that I left it unanswered.

(55) Namely, of a Sunday.

(56) I was the Doctor. She was, with all her good will, only my assistant.

(57) He had already once travelled this way, and knew better than I, what might happen to me.

(58) Provost Jorgen Sverdrup, a man of an enlightened mind, possessed much solid knowledge, and a noble, warm, and faithful

heart. He was in Greenland six years before me, and remained there some years after me. I owe very much to him, and his disinterested friendship. I learned, particularly from him, and by attending to his performance of his functions, what it was to be a minister in Greenland. In Norway he did good, and spread happiness, as he had done in Greenland. Summoned home, he enjoys now the blessed reward of fidelity.

(59) A little town on the north point of Jutland.

(60) Fishing villages on the north coast of Zealand; the latter about a mile and a half from Elsinore.